The Basel II Rating

The Basel II Rating

Ensuring Access to Finance for Your Business

MARC B. LAMBRECHT

Routledge
Taylor & Francis Group

LONDON AND NEW YORK

First published 2005 by Ashgate Publishing

Published 2016 by Routledge
2 Park Square, Milton Park, Abingdon, Oxon OX14 4RN
711 Third Avenue, New York, NY 10017, USA

Routledge is an imprint of the Taylor & Francis Group, an informa business

British Library Cataloguing in Publication Data
Lambrecht, Marc
  The Basel II rating: ensuring access to finance for your
  business
  1. Credit ratings 2. Business enterprises - Finance
  I. Title
  658.1'526

Library of Congress Cataloging-in-Publication Data
Lambrecht, Marc.
  The Basel II rating: ensuring access to finance for your business / by Marc B. Lambrecht. --1st ed.
      p. cm

1. Credit ratings. 2. Business enterprises--Finance. I. Title: Basel II rating. II Title
  HG3751.5.L36 2005
  658.15'26--dc22

2004023602

ISBN 9780566086533 (hbk)

Contents at a Glance

Contents Navigator

Figures, Panels and Tables

PART III   Passing the Test : Step Two – Drawing the Financial Conclusions

PART IV   Passing the Test: Step Three – Presenting Your Credentials

CHAPTER 1 *Introduction*

Why this book and for whom?

If your position involves any responsibility for keeping your company supplied with funds from banks and other sources, this book is for you, because Basel II vitally determines your chances of success. The book tells you how to discharge that responsibility under the changed conditions. In particular, it addresses this problem:

> *Brought down to practical terms, Basel II means that your key to bank finance, whether in the form of debt or equity investment, will be a risk rating of your business. But Basel II does not spell out the criteria you have to meet in order to pass that test or optimise its result.*

The book provides you with a methodical approach to solving the problem:

- It enables you to identify the criteria by which your bank will endeavour to establish what Basel II terms your *Probability of Default*. But the emphasis is on proactively providing your raters with the only truly effective answer, a coherent and cogent argument of your *Probability of Success*.
- While addressing the immediate need to deal with the problem of changed conditions, the book does not lose sight of the core problem of financing which remains unchanged and is basic also to Basel II: the necessity of convincing your bankers, and any provider of finance for that matter, that their money is safe with you.
- An important aspect of preparing you for a rating is the cost, time and effort to be invested. The book takes a decidedly pragmatic view of requirements and guides you in systematically maximising the score.
- The book answers the need among business people and their advisors for a practical work book. Its conciseness is deliberate. Apart from exposing the rationale of the rating process and helping you argue your case accordingly, it aims to serve you as a compendium as well as a checklist of requirements.

Certain conditions created by Basel II pose serious threats to business unless purposefully confronted and adjusted to. The following, in particular, have shaped the mission of this book.

BASEL II AFFECTS ALL FORMS OF FINANCE WORLDWIDE

The international accord colloquially referred to as Basel II sets new rigorous standards of risk management in banking. As a consequence, your banker will be obliged to apply commensurately stringent criteria in assessing the risk of financing your business.

However, the impact of Basel II goes far beyond institutional banking. It marks the beginning of a new financial culture pervading all forms of finance and funding on a global scale. Whether or not the regime of Basel II is enforced by law, no lender or investor handling other people's money can henceforth afford to apply lesser standards.

In future, therefore, no business depending for its existence on outside finance can hope to survive, let alone prosper, without making the principles of Basel II elementary to its own financial management. This universal application defines the scope of the book.

RISK RATING – THE INESCAPABLE ORDEAL

Basel II aims to make the standards of risk management applied by individual banks controllable and internationally compatible. To that end, it requires every exposure in excess of one million euros to be 'rated', that is, placed in one of a set of categories denoting different levels of risk. Each rating decision is to be conclusively documented and periodically reviewed.

Nor can requests for finance below the one million euro mark safely expect to escape some form of risk rating. Indications are that bankers tend to apply their new methods of risk mitigation also to exposures below the one million euro threshold, even especially so. In fact, most rating casualties so far seem to have occurred in that sector. At the same time, it is well to remember that bankers, too, are business people. They are happy, even keen, to do business with you and appreciate every effort on your part to make it possible for them.

Naturally, when thinking of rating, the names of specialists such as Moody's and Standard & Poor's come to mind. They are usually associated with truly large companies whose issues of equity and debt are listed on major exchanges. Obviously, you cannot be expected to mount an analysis of nearly comparable scope and depth for every financing project – nor can your bankers. The practical constraints dictate a pragmatic approach which is a guiding principle of this book.

MORE SYSTEMATIC ANALYSIS, LESS HUMAN JUDGEMENT

The question of whether you will be able to meet your obligations under a financing arrangement is an obvious one to exercise your banker's mind. The new aspect brought into it is that the question requires a formal answer. Within a framework of general criteria Basel II leaves it to each bank to develop its own approach to rating, but rating always implies a rating *system*.

This absence of clear-cut evaluation criteria is a major practical problem. You know that the bits of information you are asked to provide are critical inputs, but you have no way of knowing how each is processed in the 'black box' of a bank's proprietary system. How, then, can you make sure that the system interprets your information correctly and in the right context?

The answer is not passively to endure a rating, but to engage your raters in a constructive dialogue. The book helps you prepare the arguments enabling you to enter that dialogue with confidence.

MANY METHODS AND NONE TRULY OBJECTIVE

Although Basel II does not specify the methods of risk assessment that may be used to drive a bank's rating system, it makes frequent reference to professional rating agencies, especially Moody's and Standard & Poor's, for purposes of illustration. Credit rating does, of course, have a long tradition and there is a large body of relevant literature.

Sampling the considerable variety of methods you may despair of your chances of adequately anticipating the requirements of the rating system used by any particular bank. But all rating systems have the purpose of assessing your risk potential and all draw their inputs from a common information base. The book plan outlined at the end of this introduction gives you an impression of the major categories of information involved.

An inherent problem of risk rating is that no method will be perfectly objective. Not all the input data is quantitative. Much is qualitative and opens considerable scope for subjective interpretation and argument. The book shows you how to use that scope to best advantage.

NOT A SMALL PROBLEM: COMMUNICATING YOUR CONVICTIONS

For your forecasts of performance to convince, it will take more than those selective bits of information that typically make up company prospectuses and business plans. You will need to put your case in a logical sequence of arguments which leaves no gaps preventing a critical audience from following you.

The book guides you step by step through the process of building a seamless line of argument. Answering, in particular, the raters' questions in four major areas of investigation it will:

1   identify your success potential;
2   define your strategy for realising that potential;
3   translate the strategy into a financial plan; and
4   specify your financial requirements resulting from that plan.

Last, but by no means least, you will need an effective way of communicating your arguments. Surprisingly many firms fail to pass the scrutiny of potential funders not because they are intrinsically unsound, but because their propagators lack the ability to 'sell' their prospects. The book guides you in designing business plans and similar statements for the specific purpose of creating confidence on the part of your bankers and raters.

How to use this book

This book is written for practical purposes. It has three levels of application:

OVERVIEW OF REQUIREMENTS

The book provides you with a concise, yet comprehensive, outline of the requirements to be met for a Basel II rating.

The text is organised in tiered sections under descriptive headings so that the contents pages afford you a quick overview of the relevant issues. The depth of headed subdivision makes it easy for you to navigate the text by the list of contents.

COMPENDIUM AND CHECKLIST

The book explains the rationale of the individual requirements and guides you in a pragmatic approach to preparing the relevant information.

It is most unlikely that all the issues discussed in the book are relevant to the specific circumstances of your business. The sectional organisation of the text allows you to skip the irrelevant items which speeds up your perusal of the text and facilitates the compilation of a customised checklist of requirements.

MANUAL FOR A SELF-RATING

After an introduction to Basel II, its history, intentions and requirements, the book takes you step by step through a process that evaluates the success potential and risk of your enterprise leading up to a quantification of the results.

In this, the book does not follow the specific approach of any particular bank or rating agency. The aim is to equip you with a rational assessment of your likely performance in any rating test. The book demonstrates that this important orientation can be obtained with a minimum of effort.

Whether you are a prospective entrepreneur preparing a start-up or an executive in need of a quick preview before committing your company to a fully fledged project, the book is a fast and practical way of coming to terms with Basel II.

From purpose to plan

A structured approach to dealing with Basel II requirements

Part I   **Basel II Overview: More Questions than Answers**
Objectives and History
New Rules and the Consequences
In Search of Guidance
Confronting the Raters

Part II   **Passing the Test: Step One – Defining Your Business Strategy**
The Task Outlined
The Elements of Your Strategy
Strategic Fundamentals: Products and Markets
Your Strategic Portfolio
Rating Your Prospects
Strategic Consequences

Part III   **Passing the Test: Step Two – Drawing the Financial Conclusions**
The Task Outlined
Accounts: The Conventional Framework
Income and Liquidity: The Dual Focus of Analysts
Instruments of Financial Navigation
A Rational Look at Your Financial Future
Rating Your Financial Stability and Performance

Basel II Overview: More Questions than Answers

2 *Objectives and History*

Basel II is an accord between the banks and their national supervisors. It was developed by the Committee on Banking Supervision hosted by the Bank for International Settlements (BIS) in Basel. Its present and, for the time being, final version was published in June 2004 on the BIS website www.bis.org. As per its opening paragraph:

> *This report presents the outcome of the Basel Committee on Banking Supervision's ("the Committee") work over recent years to secure international convergence on revisions to supervisory regulations governing the capital adequacy of internationally active banks. ... The present paper is now a statement of the Committee agreed by all its members. ... This Framework and the standard it contains have been endorsed by the Central Bank Governors and Heads of Banking Supervision of the Group of Ten countries. (1)*[*]

Basel II aims to make banking safer and more profitable, especially by removing competitive inequalities. It does not advise banks on how to adjust to the new regimen. Consequently, perusing the copious documentation of the Basel proceedings will yield little of practical relevance to your search for finance. The overview included here is intended chiefly to help you understand the change in your bankers' attitude towards you and your business.

The Basel Committee on Banking Supervision was established in 1975 by the bank governors of the Group of Ten (G-10). The appointees to the Committee are senior representatives of the bank supervisory authorities and central banks of the Benelux countries (Belgium, the Netherlands and Luxembourg), Canada, France, Germany, Italy, Japan, Sweden, Switzerland, the United Kingdom and the United States.

As a group, banks perform a function of singular political importance in that they determine the amount of money circulating through the economy. This is why they operate under the strict supervision of a public authority which, in many countries, is the national reserve bank. As individual enterprises, banks carry on the business of distributors, that is, wholesalers and retailers of funds: they borrow funds to lend them out for a profit margin on interest. To protect their creditors, banks are generally required by law to maintain a level of own means relative to their lendings which their supervisory authorities consider an adequate insurance against some of their debtors defaulting. By this legal constraint a bank's lending volume is effectively limited to a certain multiple of its equity. Differences in capital charges create competitive inequalities especially for internationally active banks. From the outset, a priority objective of the Basel Committee was to redress these inequalities by harmonising the standards of capital adequacy to be observed by banks across the jurisdiction of its member countries.

---

[*] Quotes from the published text are followed by the respective number of the source paragraph in brackets.

The effort of the Committee resulted in the accord of June 1988 entitled *International Convergence of Capital Measurement and Capital Standards* and generally referred to as the Basel Capital Accord (also as Basel I). The accord which became effective at the end of 1992 stipulated a 'target standard ratio' of unencumbered capital to risk weighted assets of 8%. Although primarily aimed at internationally active banks in the G-10 countries, it has since become a quasi-international standard applied throughout the world not only to internationally active banks, but, in many countries, to domestic banks as well. The Committee's press release of 26 June 2004 announcing the agreement on the new capital accord mentions that the 1988 accord 'is believed to have been adopted in some form by more than 100 countries'.

Since then, internationalisation of business, now more aptly termed globalisation, has advanced in leaps and bounds. For internationally active banks with globally expanding asset portfolios this necessitated new approaches to risk management. One of the innovative ways devised by banks to make their exposure to risk more manageable is 'securitisation'. This is the practice of packaging several compatibly structured assets into one legally defined tranche and issuing participating claims against it to other financial institutions. As reliable measures of risk in this and other contexts, the broad asset classes by which risk weights were assigned by the 1988 accord were fast losing practical relevance. They were proving increasingly unsatisfactory also for judging the adequacy of a bank's capital base. In recognition of this, the Basel Committee proposed a new framework of capital adequacy based on more sensitive and, thus, more realistic measures of risk *(5)*. It outlined the principles of its proposal in a consultative document entitled *A New Capital Adequacy Framework* in June 1999. The Committee referred to the framework as *The New Basel Capital Accord* which the interested public dubbed Basel II.

In recognition of the international acceptance of the Basel I standard, the Committee invited comments not only from banks and bank supervisors in the G-10 countries but from major banks all over the world. Subsequently two more consultative documents were issued in January 2001 and in April 2003 reflecting the results of impact studies conducted along the way. Due to the Committee's outgoing consultative policy the new standard of Basel II not only enjoys unanimous endorsement by its members but a broadly based support in the international banking sector.

3 New Rules and the Consequences

The structure of Basel II rests on the 'Three Pillars' so called by the Committee, namely:

Pillar 1   Minimum capital requirements
Pillar 2   Supervisory review process
Pillar 3   Market discipline.

Only the first pillar will concern us here since it contains the rules governing the credit rating of bank customers which is the central topic of this book.

Approaches to rating your risk

The central instrument by which Basel II aims to realise its concept of risk-sensitive asset weighting is credit rating. Credit risk is the risk of borrowers failing to pay interest and repay principal on the dates agreed. More specifically, and in terms of Basel II, credit risk is the borrower's 'Probability of Default' (PD), where default is defined as follows:

> *A default is considered to have occurred with regard to a particular obligor when either or both of the two following events have taken place.*
> * *The bank considers that the obligor is unlikely to pay its credit obligations to the banking group in full ...*
> * *The obligor is past due more than 90 days on any material credit obligation to the banking group ... (452)*

Its definition as probability gives risk an objective, that is, statistically quantifiable, dimension. The quantification enables the derivation of risk weights by which to adjust the assets that enter the calculation of a bank's minimum capital requirement.

The traditional practice of credit rating is to assign borrowers or assets to risk categories conveniently calibrated for the practical purposes of risk evaluation and risk management.

Throughout the text of the accord Basel II makes abundantly clear that by its use of the terms credit assessment or credit rating it implies professional standards compatible with those of established rating institutions. The Committee initiated a study of professional rating practice published in a working paper entitled *Credit Ratings and Complementary Sources of Credit Quality Information* in August 2000.

Worldwide, the largest rating institutions are Moody's and Standard & Poor's, operating in their current form since 1962 and 1941, respectively. The definitions of their rating categories which are broadly compatible have set a standard adopted by most rating agencies throughout the world.

Conventions of categorising credit risk

Borrower or asset attributes for example	Moody's	S & P
Investment grade		
Premium quality, compatible with first rate sovereign issues	Aaa	AAA
High quality, but some sensitivity to world economic conditions	Aa 1 Aa 2 Aa 3	AA + AA AA -
Good quality, but sensitive to cyclical downturns in the domestic economy	A 1 A 2 A 3	A + A A -
Medium quality, susceptible to changes in market environments	Baa 1 Baa 2 Baa 3	BBB + BBB BBB -
Speculative grade		
Currently able to meet obligations, but unlikely to withstand aggressive competition	Ba 1 Ba 2 Ba 3	BB + BB BB -
Highly speculative, high dependence on uncertain developments, high potential of loss at default	B 1 B 2 B 3	B + B B -
Unable to meet obligations, high danger of default, requires financial restructuring to survive	Caa Ca C	CCC + CCC CCC -

Panel 1

For purposes of illustration Basel II uses Standard & Poor's notation throughout, emphasising that its choice implies no preference for the notation or the institution *(50, footnote 13)*.

Rating subjects

Through Basel II, systematic risk rating becomes the obligatory foundation of all lending or investment decisions made by banks. By its rules, rating has a dual focus: it estimates the risk of an exposure not only by relevant attributes of the borrower but also by those of the associated facility:

> *For corporate ... exposures, each borrower and all recognised guarantors must be assigned a rating and each exposure must be associated with a facility rating as part of the loan approval process. ... (422)*

> *Each separate legal entity to which the bank is exposed must be separately rated. ... (423)*

Basel II does not expect every bank to be able to set up an internal rating system meeting its high quality standards by the time the transition period for implementing the new framework expires at the end of 2006 *(2)*. Banks are, therefore, offered two optional approaches:

> *The Committee proposes to permit banks a choice between two broad methodologies for calculating their capital requirements for credit risk. One alternative will be to measure credit risk in a standardised manner, supported by external credit assessments. (50)*

> *The alternative methodology, which is subject to the explicit approval of the bank's supervisor, would allow banks to use their internal rating systems for credit risk. (51)*

The first option is called the Standardised Approach and the second the Internal Rating Based (IRB) Approach. There can be no doubt, however, that Basel II favours the IRB Approach, and, within that approach, the more advanced variety. Banks adopting the advanced approaches benefit by generally lower capital requirements.

The ratings obtained by either of the two basic approaches are processed into risk weights applied to the rated exposure. The bank's capital requirement is then calculated on the sum of its risk weighted assets *(44, 45)*.

For the purposes of rating Basel II distinguishes five major classes of banking-book exposures *(215)* summarised overleaf. The corporate class is subdivided into five sub-classes *(218–228)* and the retail class into three sub-classes *(231–233)*.

The scope of Basel II borrower rating

Major classes of exposure to risk

- **Corporate** – in general, debt obligations of corporations, partnerships or proprietorships in excess of 1 million euros. For special lending, typically to 'special purpose entities', see the sub-classes below.
- **Sovereign** – including reserve banks, certain development banks and other public sector entities.
- **Bank** – banks and securities firms operating under a supervisory authority.
- **Retail** – see the definition by sub-classes below.
- **Equity** – direct and indirect ownership interests, voting or non-voting, in assets and income of commercial or financial enterprises.

Corporate exposures
Sub-classes for special lending

- **Project finance** – usually for large, complex and expensive installations such as power plants, chemical processing plants, mines, transportation infrastructure, environment, telecommunications infrastructure.
- **Object finance** – in respect of physical assets such as ships, aircraft, satellites, railcars, fleets.
- **Commodities finance** – for reserves, inventories, or receivables of exchange-traded commodities such as crude oil, metals or crops.
- **Income-producing real estate** – such as office buildings to let, retail space, multifamily residential buildings, industrial or warehouse space, hotels.
- **High-volatility commercial real estate** – commercial real estate the value of which depends on conditions that are unpredictably volatile by nature.

Retail exposures
Sub-classes

- **Exposures to individuals** – such as revolving credits and lines of credit (for instance, overdrafts and credit cards), personal term loans and leases such as instalment loans and car leases.
- **Residential mortgage loans** – including first and subsequent liens, term loans and home equity lines of credit.
- **Loans to small businesses** – where the bank's total exposure to the business is less than 1 million euros.

Panel 2

It is important to note that Basel II includes equity investments among the five major classes of banking-book exposures. The definition includes 'debt obligations and other securities, partnerships, derivatives and other vehicles with the intent of conveying the economic substance of equity ownership' *(237)*. Basel II applies to banks on a consolidated basis which means that, besides integrated investment units, bank-controlled investment companies also fall under its risk assessment framework *(24)*, as do so called 'captive' investment funds managed on behalf of a bank by a specialist organisation.

The inclusion of retail exposures as a class of its own is an outcome of the consultation process the Basel Committee initiated with its first consultation paper in June 1999. The proposals contained in that paper do not include such a class as requiring separate treatment in establishing capital adequacy. The reason for including it among the revised proposals of the second consultation paper in January 2001 is mainly one of administrative economy. By its definition, large numbers of small exposures with compatible risk features can be combined in suitably demarcated pools for summary treatment in the calculation of capital requirements and the purposes of risk management.

In the retail class it is not the individual exposure that is rated for credit risk, but the individual pool of exposures. Also there is no distinction between borrower rating and facility rating as in the other classes. This pragmatic approach to retail exposures would seem to indicate a more lenient treatment of small borrowers such as individuals and small businesses. However, Basel II requires that the segmentation of a bank's retail portfolio reflects distinctive risk characteristics. Consequently bankers will still need to apply adequate credit scoring methods to assign an individual borrower to the appropriate pool. We shall return to this subject in the context of small business later on.

Weighing collateral against risk

An important factor in assessing credit risk is the availability of collateral. Collateral can significantly affect a borrower's overall credit standing. The eligibility of any collateral offered is, therefore, a major consideration for potential borrowers as well as their bankers.

The effective measure of risk mitigation is obtained by risk-weighting the individual collateral instrument. In the treatment of collateral, banks using the Standardised Approach to rating may opt for either the 'Simple Approach', which substitutes the risk weighting of the collateral for the risk weighting of the collateralised portion of the exposure, or the 'Comprehensive Approach', which effectively reduces the exposure amount by the value of the collateral *(121, 129, 130)*. The collateral eligible for risk mitigation under these two subsidiary approaches, which includes financial instruments *(145, 146)*, guarantees *(189f)* and physical assets *(72, 74)*, is summarised overleaf.

Eligible Collateral
for banks adopting the standardised method of calculating capital requirements

under the Simple Approach
- **Cash** as well as certificates of deposits and similar instruments.
- **Gold**
- **Rated[1] debt securities** issued by sovereigns or public sector entities rated at least BB-, or by other entities such as by banks and securities firms rated at least BBB-. Also short-term debt instruments rated at least A-3/P-3[2].
- **Non-rated debt securities** issued by banks which are listed on a recognised stock exchange and classified as senior debt.
- **Equities** including convertible bonds which are included in a main index.
- Mutual funds and UCITS[3] if prices of units are quoted daily.
- **Guarantees/credit derivatives** issued by sovereigns, public sector entities, banks with lower risk weight than the secured exposure, and other guarantors rated at least A-.
- **Residential real estate**.
- **Commercial real estate** with certain qualifications.

under the Comprehensive Approach (in addition to the above)
- **Equities** including convertible bonds which are not included in a main index but which are listed on a recognised exchange;
- **Mutual funds and UCITS[3]** which include such equities.

for banks adopting the internal rating based method of calculating capital requirements

under the Foundation Approach (in addition to the above)
- **Guarantees/credit derivatives** issued by corporate issuers not externally rated[1], but internally rated to be at least A- equivalent.
- **Receivables** meeting certain minimum requirements.
- **Physical collateral** (other than real estate) meeting certain minimum requirements.

under the Advanced Approach no restrictions by eligibility criteria

---

1 by a recognised external credit assessment institution
2 Moody's and Standard & Poor's notation for short-term instruments
3 Undertakings for Collective Investments in Transferable Securities

Panel 3

For IRB banks adopting the subsidiary 'Foundation Approach' the definition of eligible collateral is extended beyond the instruments listed above to special instruments, known as IRB collateral, that meet certain minimum requirements. These include receivables as well as physical collateral such as specified commercial and residential real estate *(289)*. Under the 'Advanced Approach' the more sensitive risk weighting techniques obviate eligibility criteria, and banks are free to accept any collateral of their choice.

To take account of special risks associated with a particular collateral instrument bankers are directed to apply commensurate adjustments (so called 'haircuts'), for example in cases where the market value of an instrument must be expected to fluctuate significantly or where a maturity mismatch or currency mismatch exists between the instrument and the exposure it is intended to collateralise *(e.g. 130)*. The eligibility of a collateral instrument is further circumscribed by criteria of legal certainty for ease of liquidation *(117)*.

Generally, Basel II sets high standards for assessing and monitoring the risk mitigating capacity of accepted collateral to enable speedy liquidation in the event of the secured exposure defaulting.

Standards for raters and rating

As regards the quality standards of credit rating there is, of course, no difference between the Standardised and the Internal Rating Based Approach, and relevant directions given in the context of one may be read as equally applying to the other.

Concerning the Standardised Approach, which involves employing the services of external credit assessment institutions (ECAIs), Basel II states six general criteria of eligibility *(90, 91)*.

Quality standards for Basel II raters
Eligibility criteria for external rating institutions

- **Objectivity** – A rigorous and systematic methodology subject to validation by historical evidence.
- **Independence** – An organisation unaffected by political or economic pressures and free from conflicting interests.
- **International access / transparency** – Accessibility of individual assessments to both domestic and international institutions on equal terms and the public availability of the general methodology used.
- **Disclosure** – The supply of specific information on assessment methodologies used and the actual default rates experienced by rating category.
- **Resources** – The ability to perform high-quality assessments incorporating qualitative as well as quantitative aspects, in particular, through ongoing contacts at senior and operational levels within the assessed entities.
- **Credibility** – (In addition to what is already implied in the aforestated criteria.) Customer references in respect of performance and conduct as well as internal safeguards against misuse of confidential information.

Panel 4

National bank supervisors will decide whether an ECAI is eligible for performing Basel II ratings or not. As a general rule, banks are directed to use solicited rather than unsolicited ratings from eligible ECAIs *(108)*. This means that a customer cannot rely on a published or self-initiated rating by an ECIA to be accepted for the purpose. Exceptions from this rule are in the discretion of the supervisor. Banks will not be allowed to 'cherry-pick' the assessments provided by different ECAIs *(395)*. Supervisors will also direct the 'mapping' of the assessment categories used by ECAIs to the risk weights applying under the Basel II risk weighting framework *(92)*.

Obviously, the same stringent criteria which determine the eligibility of an external rating agency will guide the supervisors when scrutinising a bank's internal rating system for approval. These and other measures render the rating process highly resistant to attempts by interested parties to influence the outcome.

Rating procedures cannot, of course, ever be free of an element of human intervention. Many inputs are qualitative in nature and, of necessity, subjective. Even quantitative processes may require judgmental inputs. Basel II recognises that human judgement is essential to any form of rating and explicitly aims to prevent an undue reliance on mechanistic method. So in the context of scoring models:

> *... Credit scoring models and other mechanical procedures are permissible as the primary or partial basis of rating assignments, and may play a role in the estimation of loss characteristics. Sufficient human judgement and human oversight is necessary to ensure that all relevant and material information, including that which is outside the scope of the model, is also taken into consideration, and that the model is used appropriately. ... The bank must have procedures for human review of model-based rating assignments.... (417)*

Consequently, there will always remain a potential for human error as well as deliberate manipulation. Basel II strives to minimise that potential by imposing strictly supervised operational rules.

> *Rating assignments and periodic rating reviews must be completed or approved by a party that does not directly stand to benefit from the extension of credit. Independence of the rating assignment process can be achieved through a range of practices that will be carefully reviewed by supervisors... (424)*

> *Banks must have independent credit risk control units that are responsible for the design or selection, implementation and performance of their internal rating systems. The unit(s) must be functionally independent from the personnel and management functions responsible for originating exposures... (441)*

> *For rating assignments based on expert judgement, banks must clearly articulate the situations in which bank officers may override the outputs of the rating process, including how and to what extent such overrides can be used and by whom. For model-based ratings, the bank must have guidelines and processes for monitoring cases where human judgement has overridden the model's rating, variables were excluded or inputs were altered. These guidelines must include identifying personnel that are responsible for approving these overrides. Banks must identify overrides and separately track their performance. (428)*

The conclusion to draw from this emphasis on the integrity of the rating process is this:

> In future, lending and investment decisions are less likely to be swayed by accommodating dispositions of bank executives towards individual customers.
>
> Basel II categorically denies borrowers a favoured status not grounded on objectively validated risk assessments.

4 *In Search of Guidance*

Obscure implications

It is an elementary tenet of business economics that every profit-oriented enterprise will use bank credit of some kind. As we shall see later, not to do so would imply an irrational sacrifice of profit potential and, hence, managerial incompetence. It is more than likely, therefore, that your firm will, sooner rather than later, be due for a Basel II rating of some kind. It is equally likely that contemplating the prospect two questions will be foremost in your mind:

- What specific information will your bankers require for the rating?
- What precisely can you do to ensure the most favourable outcome?

Unfortunately, Basel II has no clear-cut answers to these questions. It requires banks to have well defined rating criteria, but leaves it to them to specify any detail regarding them in cooperation with their supervisors.

> *A bank must have specific rating definitions, processes and criteria for assigning exposures to grades within a rating system. The rating definitions and criteria must be both plausible and intuitive and must result in a meaningful differentiation of risk... (410)*

As regards the information to be supplied by customers, Basel II merely states:

> *To ensure that banks are consistently taking into account available information, they must use all relevant and material information in assigning ratings to borrowers and facilities. Information must be current. The less information a bank has, the more conservative must be its assignments of exposures to borrower and facility grades or pools. An external rating can be the primary factor determining an internal rating assignment; however, the bank must ensure that it considers other relevant information. (411)*

On the subject of rating criteria Basel II contains nothing more specific. Considering the thorough study of rating methods and their practical performance undertaken in preparation of the new accord, it would seem that at some time in the course of its consultations, the Committee decided not to involve itself in questions of methodology as a matter of policy. It confines itself to specifying the desired results, not the methods by which to obtain them.

> *The overarching principle behind these requirements is that rating and risk estimation systems and processes provide for a meaningful assessment of borrower and transaction characteristics; a meaningful differentiation of risk; and reasonably accurate and consistent*

quantitative estimates of risk. … It is not the Committee's intention to dictate the form or
operational detail of banks' risk management policies and practice. … (389)

In the circumstances it is of some interest to look at the broad outline of rating criteria included as paragraph 265 in the second consultative document of January 2001 under the heading *Criteria on risk assessment of a borrower*, but omitted from the third consultative document of April 2003. It is quoted here in full with key phrases emphasised in bold:

Banks should take all relevant information into account in assigning ratings to a borrower.
This information should be current. The methodologies and data used in assigning ratings
should be clearly specified and documented. As a minimum, a bank should look at each of
the following factors for each borrower:

- **historical and projected capacity** *to generate cash to repay its debts and support*
  other cash requirements, such as capital expenditures required to keep the borrower a
  going concern and sustain its cash flow;
- **capital structure** *and the likelihood that unforeseen circumstances could exhaust its*
  capital cushion and result in insolvency;
- **quality of earnings**, *that is, the degree to which its revenue and cash flow emanate*
  from core business operations as opposed to unique and non-recurring sources;
- **quality and timeliness of information about the borrower**, *including the*
  availability of audited financial statements, the applicable accounting standards and
  its conformity with the standards;
- *degree of operating leverage and the resulting* **impact that demand variability**
  would have on its profitability and cash flow*;*
- *financial flexibility resulting from its* **access to the debt and equity markets** *to gain*
  additional resources;
- **depth and skill of management** *to effectively respond to changing conditions and*
  deploy resources, and its degree of aggressiveness vs. conservatism;
- *its position* **within the industry and future prospects***; and*
- *the* **risk characteristics of the country** *it is operating in, and the impact on the*
  borrower's ability to repay (including transfer risk), where the borrower is located in
  another country and may not be able to obtain foreign currency to service its debt
  obligations.

We have noted the exacting quality standards Basel II applies in judging the eligibility of external rating agencies as well as the adequacy of the banks' internal rating operations. Possibly the Committee subsequently considered the listing of the criteria unnecessary seeing that they are elementary to any professional approach to rating, as we shall find confirmed later on. In any case, the conclusion is unambiguous:

As it stands, Basel II is not a source of specific information to guide entrepreneurs and business executives in their task of preparing their businesses for the rating prescribed by it.

A guidance of sorts – still a valuable one – can be inferred from the intentions of Basel II which are implicit in its directions to banks and bank supervisors.

Controlled compliance

Banks that opt for the Standardised Approach to risk weighting their assets will, in the main, do so because they are not yet ready to tackle the onerous task of installing and operating their own rating system to the exacting standards decreed by Basel II. Meanwhile the onus of meeting those standards devolves upon external raters, especially, as these are selected with supervisory approval.

This is why Basel II is explicit about appropriate rating practice mainly in the context of the Internal Rating Based Approach. Being the more beneficial of the two approaches from the banks' point of view, it is treated by Basel II somewhat like a concession a bank must show itself fit to receive.

To be eligible for an IRB approach, a bank must demonstrate to its supervisor that it meets the IRB requirements in this document, at the outset and on an ongoing basis. ... (392)

Once the IRB status is granted there is no return to the standardised procedures, unless there are fundamental changes in the bank's business.

Once a bank adopts an IRB approach for part of its holdings, it is expected to extend it across the entire banking group ... (256)

... supervisors may allow banks to adopt a phased rollout of the IRB approach across the banking group ... (257)

A bank must produce an implementation plan, specifying to what extent and when it intends to roll out IRB approaches ... over time ... (258)

Banks adopting an IRB approach are expected to continue to employ an IRB approach. A voluntary return to the standardised or foundation approach is permitted only in extraordinary circumstances, ... (261)

The major aspects of risk which Basel II requires raters to quantify and transform into risk weights are these:

... The risk components include measures of the Probability of Default (PD), Loss Given Default (LGD), the Exposure at Default (EAD), and Effective Maturity (M). In some cases, banks may be required to use a supervisory value as opposed to an internal estimate for one or more of the risk components. (211)

Basel II insists that the rating must by applied to the borrower as well as to the facility:

A qualifying IRB rating system must have two separate and distinct dimensions: ... (396)

The first dimension must be oriented to the risk of borrower default. Separate exposures to the same borrower must be assigned to the same borrower grade irrespective of any differences in the nature of each specific transaction ... (397)

The second dimension must reflect transaction-specific factors, such as collateral, seniority, product type, etc. ... (398)

As mentioned earlier, rating practice assigns the rated entity to one in a range of categories denoting different degrees of risk and usually arranged in increasing order of risk (see Panel 1 on page 12). Basel II adopts the same structural principle:

A bank must have a meaningful distribution of exposures across grades with no excessive concentrations, on both its borrower-rating and its facility-rating scales. (403)

To meet this objective, a bank must have a minimum of seven borrower grades for non-defaulted borrowers and one for those that have defaulted. ... (404)

A borrower grade is defined as an assessment of borrower risk on the basis of a specified and distinct set of rating criteria, from which estimates of PD are derived. ... (405)

Similarly for retail exposures:

... The level of differentiation for IRB purposes must ensure that the number of exposures in a given pool is sufficient so as to allow for meaningful quantification and validation of the loss characteristics at the pool level. There must be a meaningful distribution of borrowers and exposures across pools. A single pool must not include an undue concentration of the bank's total retail exposure. (409)

Lenience for small business?

The modified treatment for retail exposures has already been mentioned (see page 14). For the purposes of calculating a bank's minimum capital requirements, retail exposures are not risk weighted individually but aggregated into pools. Since the introduction of this concept by the Basel Committee in its second consultative document of January 2001 this has led to expectations that businesses indebted to a particular bank for less than one million euros, that is, numerically, the vast majority of units in the corporate business sector, might escape the rigours of a Basel II rating. However, such sweeping conclusion is unjustified. As per the directives quoted on page 13 *(422, 423)* banks are required to segment retail exposures into pools in much the same way in which other exposures are assigned to a risk category. Thus, for the individual firm, the class distinction between corporate and retail exposure is largely academic. In practical terms, the assignment to a retail pool is a form of rating.

Basel II leaves no doubt about the standards of risk discrimination which pool assignments will have to meet:

The minimum requirements set out in this document apply to all asset classes unless noted otherwise. The standards related to the process of assigning exposures to borrower or facility grades (and the related oversight, validation, etc.) apply equally to the process of assigning retail exposures to pools of homogenous exposures, unless noted otherwise. (390)

... Banks must assign each exposure that falls within the definition of retail for IRB purposes into a particular pool. Banks must demonstrate that this process provides for a meaningful

differentiation of risk, provides for a grouping of sufficiently homogenous exposures, and allows for accurate and consistent estimation of loss characteristics at pool level. (401)

The actual purpose of the retail pool concept is not to make loan approval processes for retail exposures less stringent, but to economise their subsequent processing into risk weighted assets by using pool aggregates rather than individual exposures. These economies benefit the bank, not necessarily the business firm applying for a loan.

Nor does the assignment to a retail pool mean that the borrower will not henceforth receive individual attention.

A bank must review the loss characteristics and delinquency status of each identified risk pool on at least an annual basis. It must also review the status of individual borrowers within each pool as a means of ensuring that exposures continue to be assigned to the correct pool. ... (427)

In any case, banks are under no obligation to treat business exposures below the one million euro threshold as retail exposures. On the contrary, such treatment is premised upon certain conditions, such as compatibility with the bank's established business practice and a sufficient number of exposures to constitute an adequately risk differentiated pool.

The exposure must be one of a large pool of exposures, which are managed by the bank on a pooled basis. Supervisors may choose to set a minimum number of exposures within a pool for exposures in that pool to be treated as retail ... Small business exposures below €1 million may be treated as retail exposures if the bank treats such exposures in its internal risk management systems consistently over time and in the same manner as other retail exposures. ... However, this does not preclude retail exposures from being treated individually at some stages of the risk management process .... (232)

The conclusion is this:

In principle, and considerations of size and complexity aside, business borrowers below the one million euro mark must expect to be subjected to the same kind of credit risk assessment as other business borrowers.

No period of grace

Banks have until the end of 2006 and – in respect of the more sophisticated methods of risk assessment – until to the end of 2007 fully to comply with Basel II:

The Committee expects its members to move forward with the appropriate adoption procedures in their respective countries. ... The Committee intends the Framework set out here to be available for implementation as of yearend 2006. However, the Committee feels that one further year of impact studies or parallel calculations will be needed for the most advanced approaches, and these therefore will be available for implementation as of year-end 2007. ... (2)

These dates do not, however, imply a period of grace for you as bank customer. In order to be operative by those dates, banks not only need to have the requisite procedures in place, but have all their clients passed through the rating routine. In the circumstances the implementation schedule is tight and forces banks to speed up their preparation. Not only in the G-10 countries, but virtually the world over, financial institutions have, for some time already, begun to gear up to the new accord – amid reports of a growing number of client casualties. Consequently you, the present or future bank customer, have no time to waste either.

5 *Confronting the Raters*

The preceding chapter endeavoured to squeeze from the 239 pages of the Basel II document information of some relevance to enterprises depending for their funding on banks and bank related equity investors. The collected gleanings, however, contain precious little in the way of answering the two practical questions which guided our search:

- What specific information will your bankers require for the rating?
- What precisely can you do to ensure the most favourable outcome?

Essentially, the implication of Basel II for you is that, in future, no bank will offer you financial assistance without first establishing your 'Probability of Default'. To this end it will apply a stringent rating procedure by which to place you in one of several risk categories, and, on that basis, decide whether or to what extent and under which conditions it is prepared to risk funds on you.

Basel II only states the general principles to be observed in setting up a rating system. It considers the procedural detail is as a matter to be agreed between each bank and its supervisory authority. As you approach a particular bank for finance, you will not, as a rule, know those specifics.

Our search has reliably established one condition:

> The task of making a business fit for Basel II cannot be approached in terms of compliance with clearly defined rules. Such rules do not exist, not even in the form of general directives.

Nevertheless, there is no need passively to submit to a rating. This book will show you a way of maximising your rating results by proactively assembling the information to satisfy any rating system and preparing effective arguments for engaging raters in a constructive dialogue. This should be done, of course, with due regard for the practical circumstances in which your rating takes place. These will depend on the internal organisation of the particular bank, but certain general features of the credit assessment process are common enough for you to anticipate them and shape your preparations accordingly.

When considering your strategy for confronting your raters it is well to avoid a misleading abstraction: when you speak to a bank, you speak to a banker. The distinction is significant, because whatever the bank's policy, the banker is motivated, in addition, by personal circumstances and ambitions. It is one thing to generate new business, quite another to answer for losses incurred in consequence. For that reason alone you will expect a banker looking at your project to be conservative to a fault. The surest way of motivating a banker at first contact is by a succinctly articulated outline of your project which comes straight to the points that matter most. Invariably these are your projections of return on investment and liquid assets.

In many if not most cases the first personal meeting takes place on the strength of the impression made by a preceding written communication. It may surprise you that most proposals and applications which fail do not do so because they lack merit, but because they are badly presented. The time-pressed bank executive is not inclined to wade through a lot of text in search of the critical features that might be of interest to him. Particularly de-motivating is a load of technical jargon the banker does not feel qualified to interpret.

If your request is not turned down within the first 15 minutes of the banker's attention to your introductory presentation you will have taken the first hurdle on the way towards an approval, though only the first.

There is another hurdle not always obvious to the prospective borrower and, perhaps, not meant to be. In the rarest of cases the banker you speak to is the person who alone decides your request. This is not a matter of your contact's seniority of position. An exposure of the bank in any significant amount is hardly ever the decision of a single person. It is that of a team. It is a case for the bank's credit or investment committee of which your banker is, at best, a senior member. The personal rapport you have established with the person you speak to will only go so far.

The diagram of the credit approval process (opposite) illustrates the elements of the process. Its actual organisation will, of course, depend on the bank's administrative structure and the complexity of your case.

The credit approval process

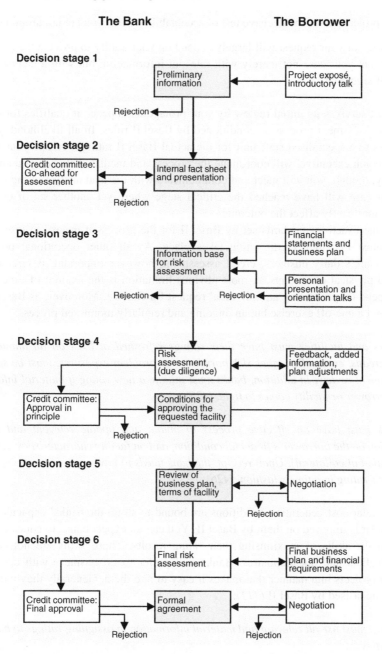

Figure 1

The important implication of the committee system is this:

> Your project passes the decisive test of acceptability when you are not around to defend it.
>
> Approval of your request will largely depend on your ability to provide the banker willing to present your case not merely with relevant information, but with a tactically effective line of argument.

If your project survives its initial review by your protagonist's peers, it qualifies for entering the bank's credit assessment process as conditioned by Basel II rules. In all likelihood, your project will now pass to a specialised staff unit for the actual Basel II rating. Perhaps your protagonist, now your account executive, will coordinate the process and mediate between you and the rating unit. Possibly, though, you will meet and communicate with the lead analyst of the rating unit in person. Your case will have reached the critical stage where yet another set of circumstantial factors can significantly affect the outcome.

Over the exacting standards set by Basel II for the process it is easy to lose sight of the practical context in which credit rating takes place. As all other operational processes that constitute a bank's daily business, credit assessment, however important, is circumscribed by financial and physical constraints. A most obvious limitation is the amount of time a bank can afford to expend on processing an individual request for finance. Moreover, as Basel II reminds us, rating is not a one-off exercise but an ongoing and regularly monitored process.

> *Borrowers and facilities must have their ratings refreshed at least on an annual basis. Certain credits, especially higher risk borrowers or problem exposures, must be subject to more frequent review. In addition, banks must initiate a new rating if material information on the borrower or facility comes to light. (425)*
>
> *The bank must have an effective process to obtain and update relevant and material information on the borrower's financial condition, and on facility characteristics ... (such as the condition of collateral). Upon receipt, the bank needs to have a procedure to update the borrower's rating in a timely fashion. (426)*

These and similar cost generating conditions are bound to strain the banks' capacity to meet the exacting standards imposed on them by Basel II. You cannot expect banks to educate prospective borrowers in the skills of maximising their rating results. Those skills are not conveyed by instruction leaflets and questionnaires. Banks will prefer to do business with customers who prepare their projects in a manner that makes it easy to rate them. Generally they will follow the old rule re-emphasised by Basel II *(411)*:

> *... banks ... must use all relevant and material information in assigning ratings to borrowers and facilities. ...*

However:

> *... The less information a bank has, the more conservative must be its assignments of exposures to borrower and facility grades or pools. ...*

In practice this means that banks will tend to make do with the information you provide as long as it is not patently unusable. Naturally, the quality of the input will be reflected in the outcome. Quality in the context of rating specifically means relevance of content and user-friendliness of presentation. Obviously, the outcome cannot improve on the substance of information provided by your data. But what can make a profound difference, and all too often does in a negative sense, is the ease with which your presentation allows raters and rating systems to absorb your information.

The possible consequences of inadequate preparation on the part of the borrower must not be underrated:

Underrepresenting your project, even if not causing it to fail the rating test outright, is likely to get it assigned to a grade below its merit.

The penalty for underrepresentation is reflected in the conditions of the desired facility, especially the rate of interest.

By no means does the need to make your information usable for a rating imply inordinate complexity. Rather, the rule – as simple as possible and as detailed as necessary – applies quite literally. This, of course, adds emphasis to the question of precisely what to do in preparation for a rating.

The remainder of the book addresses itself to that question. It outlines a practicable approach which strikes a pragmatic balance between depth and simplicity in compiling the relevant information and effectively presenting it. It serves you as a manual in doing the job yourself as it does in briefing and supervising staff or advisors.

PART II

Passing the Test: Step One – Defining Your Business Strategy

CHAPTER

6 *The Task Outlined*

There is only one way to answer your raters' preoccupation with your 'Probability of Default': it is to demonstrate your 'Probability of Success'. To minimise uncertainty, your argument needs to be more than a collection of arguments. It needs to be systematic and conclusive. Comprehensiveness is vital. In concrete terms: which operational measures and which productive resources will realise your success potential? There is a tested method by which to induce confidence in your project.

The critical issue: Your probability of success

Rating is the endeavour to measure, that is, quantify, risk. Risk is a potential that might or might not be realised in the future. In our present context, it is the potential loss incurred by your creditor or investor as a result of your enterprise failing to meet the financial targets of its business plan. Consequently, rating deals primarily with the financial future of your business. Past and present are relevant only in so far as they can be expected to modify its loss potential.

Your raters' interest will, therefore, focus on your financial plan, specifically, the projected changes in your income statement and balance sheet over the period of the bank's exposure to your business risk. Essentially, however, your financial plan is merely the translation of your business strategy into financial terms. It follows that:

> Statements made in your financial plan, such as projections of cash flow and net worth, have no significance unless shown to follow logically from an underlying strategy.

> A coherently argued strategy is the first requirement for entering the rating process.

Whatever the specific questions your raters will ask you, they have one purpose: to establish the probability of you defaulting on your obligations. With the same singularity of purpose your answers will argue the reciprocal: your probability of success.

The tested way to do that is to follow a basic scheme of causation that has universal application. Sustainable business success has two elementary roots: one is the capacity for satisfying demand in the targeted market and the other the ability to prevail against competitors as shown in the following diagram.

The root sources of business success

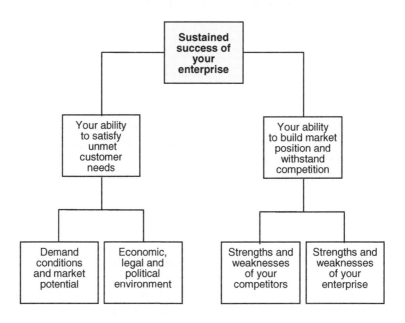

Figure 2

From the conditions on which the success of your enterprise depends derives its requirement of operational resources. The supply of resources that still needs to be obtained determines your plan of strategic action. And it is the parameters of that plan which enable you to quantify the financial prerequisites of your success in terms of kind, quantity, date and term.

Plausibility: Stand-in for objectivity

All economic activity takes place under conditions of uncertainty. Judging the future performance of a business is largely an act of speculation. The lack of factual evidence needs to be compensated by indications based on forecasts. However objective the method and inputs employed, such forecasts essentially remain statements of subjective opinion.

The confidence gap inherent in all projections of business performance cannot be closed, merely tenuously bridged, by plausibility. Plausibility is the art of rationalising. It is the more successful the more rational its approach. Simplification and generalisation impair its confidence generating power. It is an important aim of this book to help you methodically to 'objectivate' the arguments used to support your prospects of success.

A serious flaw of argumentation frequently encountered in statements made by business people to prospective funders is creating the impression that the financial requirements of their firm or project are a matter of negotiation.

It is an important element of building confidence in a funding project that the requirements are specific and that they are shown to derive with arithmetic consequence from a strategy competently designed to realise an identified business potential.

Responsibility that cannot be delegated

In the following, a catalogue of questions concerning your business strategy will give you an impression of the kind and depth of information your raters require.

People who represent the entrepreneurial leadership of an enterprise are expected to be fully conversant with its strategic and financial plan on the level of detail the rating process is meant to explore.

However much of the planning effort may be the responsibility of staff specialists and supporting personnel, it is considered a key element of management competence that the CEO or CFO of a company is able, in person and at all times, to give a reasoned account of why the company is in business and why it may be expected to succeed.

It is essentially these two central questions the raters need to obtain answers to. These answers will convince only if given by the people who personally bear the responsibility for the company's continued existence and financial success.

From arguments to argumentation

In order to make your business strategy appear plausible it is not enough to state its goals and offer arguments supporting their attainability. An argumentation aiming to convince cannot consist of a collection of contentions and assertions. It needs to follow an unbroken chain of reasoning which makes the conclusion self-evident. The format is not arbitrary. It is structured by the logic inherent in its subject.

Business success and failure being but two sides of the same coin, the logic that argues your probability of financial success is the same that defines the programme by which your rater will endeavour to assess the probability of you defaulting on your financial obligations.

Logic and scope of the rating process

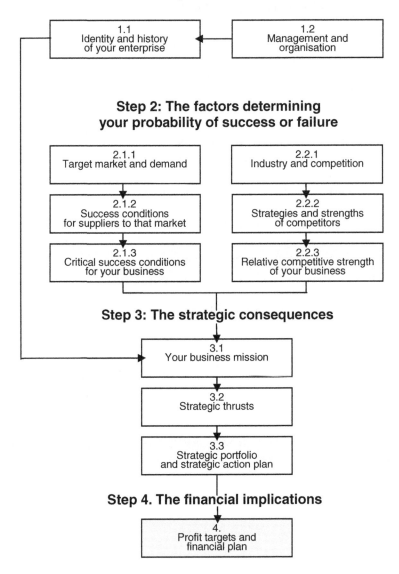

**Step 1: The operational foundations
of your business**

| 1.1
Identity and history
of your enterprise | 1.2
Management and
organisation |

**Step 2: The factors determining
your probability of success or failure**

| 2.1.1
Target market and demand | 2.2.1
Industry and competition |

| 2.1.2
Success conditions
for suppliers to that market | 2.2.2
Strategies and strengths
of competitors |

| 2.1.3
Critical success conditions
for your business | 2.2.3
Relative competitive strength
of your business |

Step 3: The strategic consequences

3.1
Your business mission

3.2
Strategic thrusts

3.3
Strategic portfolio
and strategic action plan

Step 4. The financial implications

4.
Profit targets and
financial plan

Figure 3

Translating strategy into finance

Your funders and, hence, your raters, are primarily interested in your ability to meet your financial obligations, in other words, your ability to maintain an adequate level of liquidity. Their interest in your strategy arises from their need to understand the elementary business risks of your enterprise before they can take a rational view on the likely development of your financial situation.

Once the raters are satisfied that they have a firm grasp of the operational risks of your business, the focus of their interest will shift to a critical analysis of your financial plan. Since, in all probability, your raters' professional competence will be centred in this field, it is wise to expect their financial analysis to be particularly demanding.

For this reason we shall later on devote a special section to the preparation of data required for the purpose and the methods by which raters perform their 'due diligence' on them.

7 *The Elements of Your Strategy*

It is one thing to have a strategy and another to argue it in terms at once succinct and plausible. A banker or investor will expect you to explain how you intend to create – and maintain – the conditions in which the factors of production, that is, people, processes and equipment, can be put to work with maximum efficiency. But the raters' interest goes beyond mere description. They will want to know by which mechanisms you will be able to control the productivity and, thereby, the cash generating ability of your operation.

Strategic decisions

A strategy is the systematic plan to bring about a desired result. The goal of a business strategy is the creation and sustainment of success potentials for an enterprise.

Every entrepreneurial management makes strategic decisions even if these are not expressly labelled as such. Most frequently such decisions are made in these areas:

1 The product as defined by customer needs
2 Target customer groups and target markets
3 Technology of products and production
4 Personnel, productive assets and other operational resources
5 Distinctive competences and resources for building competitive advantage
6 Functional organisation of operations
7 Long-term corporate policy.

If an enterprise consists of divisions which follow individual market strategies these may, for the purpose of strategic analysis, be treated as independent business units, irrespective of any synergistic coordination. Usually the decisive factor is the organisation under a management responsible for the unit's performance. Conversely, even though a business unit may be organised as a separate legal entity, it may not be classed as a strategic business unit, if the strategic management responsibility rests with another unit such as a parent company.

If a corporation comprises several strategic business units, the scope for strategic decisions at the parent level increases by two important dimensions:

8 Allocation of operational and financial resources to subsidiary units
9 Exploitation of synergistic potentials among the units.

The above list is not exhaustive, but all items included can be subsumed under these core principles:

> Strategic decisions have the common objective of creating, enhancing and sustaining success potential.
> They aim to achieve that objective by one or both of these approaches:
> – Maximising efficiency in meeting customer demand
> – Developing sustainable competitive advantages.

The first approach is typical for decisions regarding the adaptation of the product to customer demand, the segmentation and penetration of the market, the required operational resources and, in the case of separate business units, their allocation among them. (Items 1, 2, 3, 4 and 8.)

The second approach is directed at distinctive competences and resources by which to establish competitive advantage and the long-term corporate policy exploiting such an advantage. In the same group belong the realisation of synergies between divisions, associates and subsidiaries. (Items 5, 6, 7 and 9.)

It may be argued that strategic decisions in both these categories aim to buttress a firm's competitive strength. Identifying a segment of unmet customer needs, shaping a product to the demands of its target group, excelling in customer service and maximising cost efficiencies for attractive pricing are obvious measures to outperform existing competitors or preempt potential ones.

Yet there is an important distinction which mirrors the one made earlier when identifying the root sources of business success (see Figure 2 on page 36). Decisions in the first category, that is, those concerned with maximising the capacity of meeting customer demand, are generic to the market or the industry. Decisions in the second category aim to create a sustainable competitive advantage that is unique to your enterprise. Apart from being unique, the decisive criterion of this category is that the competitive advantage can be sustained for a strategically significant period.

The importance of sustainable competitive advantage as a determinant of business success cannot be over-emphasised. As the analysis of successful businesses reveals:

> Generic efficiencies are vital preconditions but not, on their own, sufficient guarantors of success.
>
> A record of successful performance through a period of years will invariably be related to some decisive competitive advantage that has become an enduring asset.

A typical example is a technological advantage protected by a patent. Others are the positioning in market segments protected by entry barriers or the creation of unique cost synergies by backward or forward linkages in production and distribution.

In consequence of the above, a funder or rater concerned with your ability to meet your debt obligations over the respective term or with the likelihood of receiving an adequate average return over the amortisation period of an investment will pay special attention to the distinctive competences, rights or assets that constitute the competitive advantage of your enterprise.

Strategic management

Strategic management is the craft of dealing rationally and methodically with the problems of uncertainty. In practice this means steering a business by goals of achievement, as distinct from making the best of a given set of circumstances. A market environment increasingly characterised by fast-developing opportunities and threats requires speedy responses. The traditional administrative management approach being unequal to the task, the standard today is the dynamic strategic one.

One prominent feature of strategic management is the dynamic approach to planning. As periodic planning efforts, especially the traditional yearly one, are proving inadequate, it has become necessary to introduce dynamic planning systems capable of currently adapting strategies to changing conditions. This adaptive capacity, that is, the facility to home in on a constantly moving target, has become a mark of competent risk management. Your raters will want to see proof of strategically relevant information being systematically monitored.

It is one thing to draw up a strategic plan and quite another to implement it. In this regard it is important to bear in mind two principles of practical strategic analysis that must be expected to guide a rater in his work:

> Business plans must be implemented by the people who make them.
>
> Information on business plans is trustworthy only if obtained from the people responsible for their implementation.

The ability of leading executives exhaustively to answer questions about their company's business plan is a decisive criterion in rating management competence.

STRATEGIC PLANNING

Your strategic plan identifies the measures required to implement your strategic decisions, lists the resources required and details the relevant action to be taken.

Specifically, your strategic planning effort will be directed at closing recognised 'strategic gaps', that is, prevailing shortcomings of your strategic strength relative to what is needed to realise the projected success potential of your enterprise. The planning process has three major components:

- The process begins with an analysis of the existing success potential. It identifies and, where possible, quantifies, the conditions under which the potential can be expected to be realised.
- The next step is the specification of success targets based on your judgement as to what extent the identified potential can realistically be exploited. Available or obtainable financial resources are major inputs to these considerations.
- The result of your planning effort, your strategy, is a catalogue of measures by which to create the conditions for the targeted success together with a time-critical plan of action for their implementation.

Your financial plan is the translation of your strategy into financial terms. As emphasised before: to a funder or rater no item in a financial plan makes sense unless related to a corresponding item in the underlying plan of strategic action.

STRATEGIC CONTROLLING

Strategic controlling means steering your business by the course plotted in your plan. Plans, however, deal with an unknown future, hence, cannot ever be expected to come true with any measure of certainty. This makes constant monitoring paramount.

Monitoring requires sensitive instruments comparing actual with planned performance. This is the function of your management information system. In this context, system does not imply methodical or technical sophistication, but practical efficiency. Important is the speed at which signals, especially those indicating deviations from the course, are transmitted to the navigator.

For the signals to have practical consequence they must be speedily acted upon. This presupposes that the relevant steering mechanisms are functional. A well-appointed 'controlling cockpit' is not enough. The essence of effective risk management is knowing what to do in response to a warning signal, not merely having the means to do it.

In practice, this requires you to reconsider your strategic plan at suitably frequent intervals. The routine will repetitively raise the question of whether your current plan of strategic action is still adequate to handle the situation or whether it requires adaptation to meet changed conditions. However, the periodic review will need to be more than a check on the adequacy of specific measures. It will question the continued validity of the whole strategic concept, that is, the 'mission' of your enterprise.

The importance of financial controlling in this context cannot be over-emphasised. The ability actually to implement the changes indicated by the strategic review is more often than not a matter of financial feasibility.

By the nature of their business, bankers have special competence in financial analysis, and you might find them predominantly concerned with the financial implications of your strategy. This does not mean, however, that the underlying strategic issues will receive less critical attention. It is well always to bear in mind that every item in your financial plan derives its meaning and validity from your strategy and will be judged by your raters in that context.

To assist you with effectively presenting the strategic foundations of your financial plan the salient concepts of strategic reasoning and strategic planning will be discussed in some detail in the chapters that follow.

8 *Strategic Fundamentals: Products and Markets*

Essentially, the success potential of your enterprise is defined by its market. Consequently, your business strategy is first and foremost a market strategy. It is this potential which will draw the most critical attention. There is a natural inclination for managements to base their expectations on the quality of their products rather than the quality of the demand they are meant to supply – and thereby severely damage their chances of attracting funders.

There are banks and investment companies who focus their activities on certain markets and industries. As a rule, however, you cannot expect your raters to have specialist knowledge of the operational specifics of your industry, let alone your enterprise. In particular, you will need to bear in mind that, typically, their career background is financial, not technical.

Central terms of a business strategy

At the centre of strategic considerations stands the relationship between products and their markets. Prevailing conditions of supply and demand in a particular market vitally determine the measure of success an enterprise can hope to achieve in it.

YOUR PRODUCT

In a strategic context, the term product implies not merely the physical attributes colloquially associated with the word, but any economic good produced to meet a demand. This includes non-physical attributes such as distribution and other services provided to ensure its usability in the hands of its acquirer. This means that a product with physical attributes is not necessarily 'finished' merely because it has passed the process of its manufacture. Nor is a product exhaustively defined in terms of its generic use or usefulness. Changes in design and presentation may be all that is needed to create a new product in the eyes of the user.

YOUR MARKET

By definition, a business strategy aims to satisfy the demand existing in specific markets. In this context, a market is defined as the group of potential customers, the 'target group', constituting the 'target market'. In many cases, a generic consumer need expresses itself in differing forms of demand requiring equivalently differing ways of meeting it, for instance, by adapting the same core product in terms of distribution, service or advertising. The 'segmentation' of a generic market into several demand groups necessitates an individual strategic approach to each.

CUSTOMER NEEDS AND DEMAND

Conducting a business means to satisfy customer needs – at a price. Customer needs must be enabled by purchasing power to constitute demand. That the demand for a product varies inversely with its price is an elementary principle of economics. For the purposes of market strategy yet another factor is decisive: The ability to buy must turn into the willingness to buy in order to make a sale.

Product strategy vs market strategy

In light of the above the first question about your products that require an answer is this: Do you have a product for which to find a suitable market or have you found a market which demands a product such as yours?

It is an observation frequently made by analysts of business plans that corporate strategies are product driven rather than market driven. Products are often inspired by the possibility of their production rather than an identified demand potential. This tends to be the case, in particular, with technical inventions. For an engineering-oriented management it seems to be easy to forget that products are for markets, not markets for products.

It is a common occurrence that entrepreneurs try to convince bankers and investors with impressive product technology, confronting them with elaborate documentation of technical attributes and performance tests. More often then not such attempts to create confidence in the prospects of an enterprise prove counterproductive. A strategy of product development that is not expressly and closely aligned to market demand will usually be judged to be uneconomic or downright misdirected.

Of course, instances of demand for a product having been created by skilful promotion are well known. There may conceivably be cases where such a strategy is not only possible, but even indicated. But these will always be considered as exceptions from the norm and require commensurately solid argument.

This in no way diminishes the strategic importance of innovative product technology as a prominent source of competitive advantage. The critical aspect, however, which makes technology a contributor to business success is always the economic, never the technical one.

> A business strategy is first and foremost a market strategy.
>
> It has two elementary functions:
> 1 identifying customer needs endowed with purchasing power; and
> 2 defining the product attributes and supply features capable of turning that purchasing power into buying decisions.

As a rule, it will not be the major problem to convince a funder or rater that an existing or planned product is or will be technically capable of satisfying a particular customer need. If, in this context, questions of technical product performance become relevant, the obvious way to settle them is by way of independent expert opinion. On the other hand, the future performance of a product as a contributor to the financial success of an enterprise is not a question that can be answered by outsiders. In order to convince the raters it will need to be argued by the executives responsible for their company's strategy and its implementation.

9 *Your Strategic Portfolio*

It is natural for raters to open their investigation with questions about the historical development and current situation of your business. Their interest will, of course, be concentrated on conditions that are relevant to its future performance, that is, its present stock of strategic assets. By far the most important among these is the quality of management. Therefore, the competence and experience of key personnel will be a major topic of discussion.

The existing operational facilities constitute strategic assets only in so far as they are directly relevant to the pursuit of the company's strategic goals. Typically these are staff skills, product technologies, productive equipment, administrative facilities, warehousing and distribution facilities, sources of materials, sources of services, sources of finance and the like.

The question of relevance, however, can only be answered by a detailed analysis of the company's strategy. They enter the evaluation of the company's 'strategic portfolio' mainly in the context of identifying existing strategic deficits and the finance required to close them.

In the initial phase of their investigation, raters tend to focus on conditions which cannot easily be changed and, for the purpose of analysing success and risk potentials, have to be taken as givens. These are:

- Your chosen line of business and the present subject and scope of your enterprise.
- The relevant competence of your management as the most basic success condition.
- In the case of your enterprise being connected, however loosely or closely, with other business entities, the specific constraints or benefits deriving from such connections.

The operational premise: Subject and scope

Income is generated by producing goods and services that are sold in the market. Thus, a company's products and productive activities are the most visible features of its business. What was said above about the strategic concept of product applies equally to that of production: it is a source of income only in so far as its products satisfy a market demand, which implies that the factors of production, such as staff and productive assets, are the necessary means but not the root source of business success.

A sure way of irritating your bankers or raters is to swamp them with descriptions of technical equipment or processes. They cannot be expected to have the relevant technical competence to judge the contents or even understand the jargon. You will usually find them willing to proceed on the premise that your products are technically equal to their commercial objective. At a more advanced stage of their due diligence, especially when a favourable conclusion appears likely, experts might be called in to confirm the technical premises of your strategy.

Defining a company's activities in terms of demand served rather then products supplied is not, however, a matter of communicative convenience. It is a major aspect of a company's strategic orientation in the economy. In most cases a segment of customer needs represents a greater business potential than a particular kind of product. For example, a road haulage company with a thorough understanding of their customers' transport requirements may define or redefine themselves as providers of goods transport in any suitable form, that is, extend the scope of their activities into rail, air and sea transport.

Defining the scope of your company's business activity is, thus, a fundamental strategic decision of far-reaching consequence, as will become increasingly evident in the course of our discussion.

The above notwithstanding, it may be helpful to describe your business in terms of a representative system of industrial classification. On a national level industrial classification systems are often administered by government agencies. Some have attained international recognition such as the *Standard Industrial Classification* systems (SIC) of the United Kingdom and the United States. There are also supra-national systems such as the *Statistical Classification of Economic Activity in the European Community* (CPA) and the *North American Industry Classification System* (NAICS) created for common usage in Canada, the United States and Mexico. For international application the United Nations have developed several coding systems such as the *International Standard Industrial Classification of all Economic Activity* (ISIC) and the *Central Product Classification* (CPC).

Another useful item of background information is a digest of your firm's history in order to give a succinct account of the salient events and developments which shaped its present situation. A detailed record of its financial history in the form of income statements and balance sheets will also be required for placing your current financial plan in perspective.

The quality of management

Management First! The old business wisdom reflected in this adage is given the same weight by raters as by anyone else required to pass judgement on a firm's prospects. But, since the key executives whose competence the raters are called upon to evaluate are the very people they preferably talk to and depend on for relevant information, rating the management is a somewhat delicate matter.

Nevertheless, because of the weight assigned to management competence as a factor deciding the future of an enterprise, the job needs to be done with commensurate thoroughness. In order to mitigate the inherent problems which are, first, the unavoidable element of subjectivity in rating management quality and, second, the difficulty of quantifying the result, raters are likely to follow certain structured guidelines.

Your raters' attention is likely to focus on two critical aspects of management that define the preparedness and ability to react to unforeseen events or developments: one is a company's particular management culture and philosophy and the other the constraints imposed on management by its organisational structure. In internal guidelines for raters I have found the following areas emphasised:

- **Relevant personal qualification**, for example, experience in relevant functions of management, experience of the industry, educational and occupational career, specialist knowledge and skills.

- **A strategic approach to management,** for example, the systematic identification of opportunities and risks, the setting of strategic goals, the plan of implementation.
- **An articulated financial policy**, for example, the concept of a financial structure, principles of the internal allocation of funds, the financial planning procedure, the instruments of cash flow and liquidity management, the relationships with bankers, investors and other providers of finance.
- **Rationality of decision processes**, for example, the organisation of management functions, the interaction of those functions in the decision process, the scope of individual decision responsibility, the attitude towards risk-taking, the system of checks and balances.
- **Past performance by strategic goals**, for example, in terms of market share, market penetration, competitive strength, staff motivation, productivity, profitability, liquidity.
- **Effectiveness of controlling systems**, for example, the review processes ensuring the validity of current strategic goals and the financial plan reflecting them, the efficiency of the information flow of operational and financial data, the organisation of auditing responsibilities.
- **Third party influence**, for example, overriding policies of a parent organisation, budgetary controls, allocation of funds, financial guarantees, authorisation of certain management decisions by major shareholders or banks.
- **Continuity of management**, for example, the degree of dependence on individual executives for operational efficiency, the organisation of managers in teams, provisional plans for securing replacements in emergencies and cases of illness or retirement.

Group affiliations: Support or constraint?

The influence of a parent organisation on the policy and management of its subsidiaries has already been mentioned as a factor modifying the quality of management in rating terms.

There are other, potentially more profound, consequences of group relationships, such as:

- The **relative financial situation** and strength of the parent or affiliates.
- The likelihood of **financial support** from parent or affiliates in the absence of formal agreements.
- Contractual covenants of **mutual financial support.**
- **Guarantees** and similar assurances covering the rated company's debt.
- **Maintenance agreements** regarding continuance of controlling ownership, minimum measures of financial structure, minimum coverage of expenditure by income etc.
- The extent of **legal liability of parent or affiliates** to honour the rated company's debt in the case of its default.
- Agreements or policy regarding the **allocation of group financial resources** between the members of the group.
- Agreements or policy regarding the **transfer of profits or cash** to the parent or affiliates.

The raters will need to establish in which measure group affiliations decrease or increase the funding risk represented by the rated company. Of special interest is the enforceability of claims or liabilities arising from such agreements or other legal causes.

10 *Rating Your Prospects*

As we have seen, apart from management competence, the success of your business – hence also its Probability of Default – has two main roots: its ability to satisfy a specific demand and the strength to defend its market position against competitors (see Figure 2 on page 34). Of necessity, the assessment of your market potential and your competitive strength is largely subjective. To gain acceptance, your assertions need to be founded on a thoroughly methodical analysis.

Market potential

The criteria by which to rate your ability to supply demand will be discussed in the three steps of the process:

Step one   The identification of your target markets and their demand potential.
Step two   The identification of the conditions to be met by a supplier in order successfully to exploit that demand potential.
Step three   The assessment of the extent to which your company meets the identified success conditions.

FROM CUSTOMER NEEDS TO TARGET MARKETS

There are principally three classes of questions by which to rate the success potential of your target markets:

- What are the unmet customer needs that your offer of goods and services aims to satisfy?
- Which potential demand do these customer needs represent and at which price levels can you expect them to turn into buying decisions?
- Are there major environmental influences such as economic, legal or cultural conditions that can be expected to subdue or boost demand?

Unmet customer needs

Market segmentation is the division of a market into sub-markets by criteria of demand. It has major strategic importance for companies who need to defend themselves against significantly larger competitors. By aligning your supply programme to specific features of a recognised customer need you may limit demand to a volume that comfortably matches your present or planned output, distribution and service capacities, but would be uneconomical for a competitor needing to utilise larger capacities. Demand in such 'niches' of a wider market in which specific customer needs have been neglected by large suppliers is often intense and allows the smaller competitor rapidly to build and fortify a dominant market position.

> Experience shows that market segmentation is one of the most successful strategies for small- and medium-sized enterprises. Next to an adequate financial base, it is possibly the most reliable source of market success.
>
> For that reason it is the aspect best suited to creating confidence in a firm's prospects on the part of a banker or rater.

So powerful is the success potential of segmentation that it is often also employed by large suppliers who combine economic advantages of mass production with product features designed to appeal to different segments of their market. This is sometimes taken to the point where individual units of a company appear to be in competition with each other.

However, for segmentation to be effective, the delineation of individual segments must be clearly distinctive. A segmentation by insufficiently different demand features in adjoining segments is strategically unproductive and uneconomical.

Here follows a sample of criteria by which to explore the segmentation potential of your market relative to your supply capacity:

Identifying unmet customer needs

Examples of differentiating features

Customer needs in target segments
differentiated by:
- ☐ Kind of customer, e.g. private or business, region, industry, company type and size
- ☐ Functional product features, e.g. mode of application or user type
- ☐ Product design, e.g. culture or fashion

Organisation of demand and decision paths
differentiated by:
- ☐ Typical means of customer contact
- ☐ Customary ways of negotiating purchases
- ☐ Preferred manner of placing orders
- ☐ Hierarchic decision paths in organisations
- ☐ Inclusion of third parties, e.g. consultants, in purchasing decisions

Purchase motivation
differentiated by:
- ☐ Purchasing power and propensity to spend, e.g. income or budget
- ☐ Expected benefits (rational and irrational), e.g. functionality, brand preference, price, buying habits
- ☐ Aspect of the supply process considered important, e.g. technology, service, cost of delivery
- ☐ Dissatisfaction with existing conditions of supply or supplier attitudes

Product availability
differentiated by:
- ☐ Products on offer in the market to satisfy the targeted segment of demand
- ☐ Your product offers to that target segment
- ☐ Unmet demand capable of being activated by suitably featured supply

---

Panel 5

Demand volume and prices

Having identified the distinctive demand segments targeted by your market strategy the next step is to obtain the information required to align your supply capacity and activities to the identified market potential.

Market information that is genuinely specific to a particular demand segment defined by criteria such as listed above is often not readily available. For data on that level of specification you will, in most cases, have to rely on your own market experience and/or market research.

Knowing your markets is, of course, an elementary pre-condition for conducting any business.

> Your bankers and raters will expect your knowledge of your markets to be specific and detailed enough to drive a systematic strategy of exploiting their potential.
>
> Of necessity, gaps in that knowledge correspondingly lower the degree of confidence in the effectiveness or adequacy of the measures on which your request for finance is based.

Typical questions arising in this context are these:

Demand volume and prices
Examples of relevant questions

Market size and growth
☐ The volume (in currency terms) of demand or latent demand in the target markets at present
☐ Expected growth of demand in the target markets
☐ Expected changes in demand volume due to factors such as satiation or migration to other segments

Prices
☐ Orientation on observable price levels or predominance of negotiated prices
☐ General trends towards higher or lower price levels
☐ Conditions and influences expected to influence price levels

---

Panel 6

Environmental influences on demand

There may be influences extraneous to the market that significantly affect demand conditions. Trends or expected developments in these influences may be important inputs to your strategic planning process.

Environmental influences

Economy
for example:
- ☐   Economic growth and business cycle
- ☐   Balance of payments and currency rates
- ☐   Employment/unemployment
- ☐   Financial markets and interest rates

Technology
for example:
- ☐   Mature technologies
- ☐   New technologies
- ☐   Relevant life cycles
- ☐   Government

Government
for example:
- ☐   Legislation
- ☐   Economic and financial policies
- ☐   Taxation
- ☐   Subsidies

Demography
for example:
- ☐   Age pyramid
- ☐   Income groups
- ☐   Household/family units
- ☐   Geographic distribution

Culture
for example:
- ☐   Life style
- ☐   Fashion
- ☐   Public opinion

Panel 7

GENERAL SUCCESS CONDITIONS FOR SUPPLIERS

The practical purpose of strategic planning is the specification of measures by which you expect to achieve or improve market success. For this it was necessary first to establish the demand potential of your target markets. Next, we need to establish the conditions a supplier must meet to be successful in these markets.

Although we are looking at *your* target markets, we are, at this stage, investigating the success conditions for suppliers to these markets in general, that is, without reference to the specific features of your product and your supply capacity. There are two important reasons for this approach: firstly, the mental distance from your own situation enhances the objectivity of your judgement. That objectivity, in turn, enables you to set realistic 'benchmarks' by which to rate your own success potential and calibrate 'scorecards' measuring your achievement in establishing success conditions.

To describe the attributes of the successful supplier to your target markets you should proceed as follows:

Step one   Establish the critical factors that determine success in supplying the defined markets.

Step two   From the critical success factors established compile a profile of the supplier best placed to realise the potential of those markets.

Step three   Identify the most effective measures by which suppliers can stimulate demand in the markets.

Critical success factors

The conditions most highly rated are those that establish a sustainable competitive advantage. Relative competitive advantage is most frequently established in one or more of these areas:

- Market position
- Production and service capacity
- Innovative technology
- Staff competences and skills.

Financial resources are not included in the list. This is because finance is strictly speaking not in itself a competitive advantage but the means by which to obtain or develop such advantages. One purpose of the systematic articulation of your strategy is to establish the financial requirements for implementing it. In our present context of rating, the issue of 'justifying' those requirements is, in fact, the crucial one.

The success conditions relating to your target markets are the backbone of your strategy and warrant special care in identifying them. Areas in which corporate strategies frequently recognise success factors are listed overleaf:

Success factors for supplying the target market

Market position
for example:
- ☐ Demand orientation
- ☐ Quality standards
- ☐ Product differentiation
- ☐ Visibility in target markets
- ☐ Brand and corporate image
- ☐ Promotion/public relations
- ☐ Customer relations/accessibility

Production and service capacity
for example:
- ☐ Output capacity
- ☐ Reliability of suppliers
- ☐ Prices of raw materials
- ☐ Potential for reducing costs
- ☐ Potential for increasing productivity
- ☐ Transport logistics
- ☐ Delivery terms
- ☐ Marketing support for distributors
- ☐ Distributor indemnification
- ☐ Trade finance for customers
- ☐ Technical support and maintenance services

Product and systems technology
for example:
- ☐ Product technology
- ☐ Production systems
- ☐ Technical expertise
- ☐ Development and research capacity
- ☐ Licences and patents
- ☐ Distribution systems
- ☐ Planning and controlling systems

Personal competences and skills
for example:
- ☐ Strategic planning
- ☐ Financial planning and controlling
- ☐ Research and development
- ☐ Marketing
- ☐ Production
- ☐ Distribution
- ☐ Customer relations

Panel 8

Profiling the successful supplier

Having identified the attributes that define supplier success, the next step is to rank them in order of their relative contribution to that success. Here again you will draw on your own market experience and/or the results of your market research. The following is an illustrative example assuming a selection of success factors from among those listed above. In practice, such a list of significant contributors will rarely have more than 20 entries and usually considerably fewer.

A benchmark profile such as illustrated in the following table will need to be established for each of the target markets you have defined. If, however, a larger number of success factors is common to all or several of these markets, these will conveniently be combined in summary profiles. The comments added to the success factors listed indicate the possibility of further specification.

Benchmark conditions for success in the target market
Weighted according to their relative importance

Example case

Critical success factors	Weights
1. Demand orientation especially: Market research team monitoring unmet customer needs in target markets for guiding product development and service programs	15
2. Visibility in the target market especially: Branches in geographical market centres providing distributor support and arranging trade finance	14
3. Trade finance for customers especially: Arranging trade finance for distributors and end users in cooperation with specialised financial institutions	12
4. Delivery terms especially: Inventory control integrated with production planning; own transport organisation geared to fast delivery	10
5. Quality standards especially: Strict compliance with generally accepted quality standards; exclusive use of independently certified materials	10
6. Reliability of suppliers especially: Continuity of just-in-time deliveries of critical components secured by flexible arrangements with several suppliers	9
7. Prices of raw materials especially: Constant monitoring of relevant commodity prices on international exchanges and hedging of forward purchases in the futures markets	9
8. Marketing support for distributors especially: Support of distributors by training courses for sales staff, advertising in the media and public relations events	6
9. Distributor Indemnification especially: Indemnity for distributors from claims for damages by customers backed by own insurance against production and delivery risks	6
10. Brand and corporate image especially: Creating and maintaining brand awareness by published quality tests, trade fair exhibitions and public relations events	5
11. Product technology especially: State of the art product and production technology; development and maintenance of systems and processes by a team of specialists	4
	100

Table 1

Means of controlling sales volume

A key consideration in evaluating success potential or risk is a firm's ability systematically to increase its sales. There are basically two conditions which create that ability:

1   The existence of unmet customer needs or dissatisfaction with available supplies which enables a relevantly oriented supplier to increase sales merely by increasing output.
2   The only other way of increasing sales is by stimulating additional demand.

The scope for controlling sales volume

Strategy 1: Exploiting unmet customer needs

for example:
☐   Unavailability of suitable products
☐   Available products lacking user-friendliness
☐   Low product quality
☐   Unavailable or unreliable customer service
☐   Lacking access to supplier
☐   Bad supplier image

Strategy 2: Stimulating demand

for example through:
☐   Promotion media
    e.g. advertising, mailing, trade fairs, visits by sales staff
☐   Product attributes
    e.g. technical efficiency, durability, practical design
☐   Auxiliary services
    e.g. delivery terms, credit terms, technical service
☐   Emotional appeal
    e.g. attractive design, comfort, security, prestige

Panel 9

SUCCESS CONDITIONS SPECIFIC TO YOUR FIRM

The benchmarks obtained by analysing the success conditions for suppliers to your target markets can now be used to measure the extent to which your own enterprise fulfils these conditions. The resulting measurements will be the more reliable – and credible for your raters – the more objective the derivation of the benchmarks. It will be helpful, therefore, if the general success scenario presented can be referenced to authoritative published sources or corroborated by independent experts.

From that base, the rating of the success-generating attributes of your enterprise will proceed in two steps:

Step one   Assess the degree in which your enterprise fulfils the benchmark conditions for each target market.

Step two   Evaluate your relative success profile thus obtained and note, in particular, significant deficits.

The success-generating attributes of your firm

A measure of the extent to which, in your own judgement, your enterprise fulfils the identified benchmark conditions for the target market is obtained by a simple calculation:

Fulfilment of critical success conditions by your firm in the target market

Example case

Success factors *	Weights) (Sum = 100) A	Fulfilment rate (%) B	Index A x B / 100 C
1. Demand orientation	15	80	12.0
2. Visibility in the target market	14	40	5.6
3. Trade finance for customers	12	60	7.2
4. Delivery terms	10	50	5.0
5. Quality standards	10	90	9.0
6. Reliability of suppliers	9	70	6.3
7. Prices of raw materials	9	30	2.7
8. Marketing support for distributors	6	50	3.0
9. Distributor indemnification	6	70	4.2
10. Brand and corporate image	5	20	1.0
11. Product technology	4	70	2.8
Average fulfilment of success conditions:			58.8 %

* see Table 1 on page 55

Table 2

In the case of a start-up or the planned entry into a new market, the fulfilment rates are to be interpreted as your assessment of your initial position taking into account present circumstances and available resources.

Evaluating your success profile

A rater will be looking, in particular, for any significant 'strategic gaps', that is, deficits in your strategic portfolio, because they represent your entrepreneurial risk. It is an important purpose of a strategic planning exercise to identify such gaps and state, whether they can be closed and by what means or, in case they cannot be closed, whether they can be compensated by exceeding the benchmarks in other areas.

However, the deficits showing up in the above table cannot, on the strength of this analysis alone, be interpreted as strategic gaps. You will recall that the benchmarks are meant to represent the ideal of a supplier fulfilling the success conditions of the market to an optimal extent and in an optimal combination.

In reality, your market success is significantly conditioned by competition, more specifically, by your relative competitive strength. It still remains to be established how your existing or potential competitors shape up relative to the hypothetical benchmarks. Final conclusions regarding the existence and the extent of strategic gaps will need to be reserved until the analysis of the competitive condition in your target markets has been completed. That analysis is the subject of the following section.

Competitive strength

Our discussion of strategy began with identifying the root sources of business success. They are, first, the capacity for supplying customer demand and, second, the ability to withstand competition (see Figure 2 on page 34). We have so far considered the first of the two causes and now need to complete the survey of success conditions by addressing the second.

The analysis of your competitive strength proceeds in three steps:

Step one   Collect information about your industry and the competitive conditions characterising it.

Step two   Identify major competitors (existing or potential) and assess their competitive strength.

Step three   Compare your competitive strength with that of your major competitors or that of other suppliers in the industry as a group.

INDUSTRY AND SUPPLY CONDITIONS

Market potentials attracting suppliers

The first question of relevance to our analysis is the reason why entrepreneurs are attracted to the industry.

In reality, there may be many reasons for carrying on a certain kind of industrial activity, not all of them purely economic and some not even perfectly rational. Powerful determining factors are tradition, historical developments and major investments made a long time ago, as well as the personal experience, competence and inclination of founders, shareholders, promoters or leading personalities.

In the present context, however, it is the rational reasons that might draw an entrepreneur towards your industry that interest us, because these will help us assess the possibility of new competitors entering your industry and threatening your present or targeted market share.

Here follows a selection of frequently named reasons for choosing a particular industry.

Criteria of industry attractiveness

a selection

Demand

for example:
- ☐ Size of the markets supplied
- ☐ Growth of demand
- ☐ Unmet customer needs
- ☐ Low intensity of competition
- ☐ Bargaining power of customers
- ☐ Price levels

Economies

for example:
- ☐ Earning potential
- ☐ Minimum size of organisation
- ☐ Required investments
- ☐ Availability of finance

Supplies

for example:
- ☐ Reliability of supplies
- ☐ Bargaining power of suppliers
- ☐ Price stability

Staff

for example:
- ☐ Minimum size of staff complement
- ☐ Availability of relevant skills
- ☐ Staff costs

Environment

for example:
- ☐ Sensitivity to business cycles
- ☐ Regulatory constrains
- ☐ Subsidies

Panel 10

Structural characteristics of the industry

What was said about your markets also holds in respect of your industry:

> Knowing one's industry is an essential condition of business success.
>
> Your raters will expect you, in particular, to be well informed about your competitors, especially, their strategic strengths and weaknesses.

Knowledge of your industry includes familiarity with relevant published information, notably periodically updated statistical indicators of conditions and activity. It will be useful to have an up-to-date digest of such information.

The dimensions of industry analysis will reflect the particular features of the sector you operate in, but in many cases the following will be significant.

Dimensions of industry analysis
a selection

Industry size and growth
for example:
- ☐   Output
- ☐   Employment
- ☐   Investment
- ☐   Productivity
- ☐   Growth potentials

General trends and developments
for example:
- ☐   Technological advancement
- ☐   Sensitivity to business cycles
- ☐   Changes in customer preferences

Typical operational features
for example:
- ☐   Organisation of operations
- ☐   Economies of scale
- ☐   Minimum firm size by technical criteria
- ☐   Capital-labour ratio

Organisation of distribution
for example:
- ☐   Preferred distribution channels
- ☐   Bargaining power of distributors
- ☐   Distribution costs relative to sales
- ☐   Market geography

Product life cycle
for example:
- ☐   Stage of technical maturity
- ☐   Degree of demand saturation
- ☐   Redundancy/substitution

Costs and financing
for example:
- ☐   Costs
- ☐   Investments
- ☐   Capital
- ☐   Debt

Bargaining power of customers
for example:
- ☐   Dependency on few major customers
- ☐   Ease of switching suppliers
- ☐   Tendency to build backward linkages

Bargaining power of suppliers
for example:
- ☐   Degree of dependency on individual suppliers
- ☐   Supply restrictions/quota systems
- ☐   Cartels and similar restrictions of competition

Panel 11

The common features of cost and financial structure among your peer group are of special interest to bankers and raters. They serve as benchmarks in judging your financial plan. If your peer group consists mainly of companies listed on a stock exchange, their annual financial statements will be available. Particularly useful sources of relevant information are industry surveys published by financial analysts. Other sources are industry associations such as chambers of commerce, central banks, universities and government departments of statistics.

Usually, the larger the peer group and the smaller the average size of its members in terms of balance sheet totals the less disaggregated the financial data included in such surveys. For our present purposes the level of disaggregation shown below would be desirable, but may not always be obtainable.

Typical items of comparative industry analysis

Income statement

	Sales revenue	100 %
-	Cost of sales (materials and other turnover proportional costs)	%
=	Gross profit	%
-	Overheads (administration, distribution, depreciation etc.)	%
=	Operating profit	%
-	Interest on debt	%
-	Taxes	%
=	Profit	%

Balance sheet

Investments (Assets)

	Fixed assets (e.g. buildings, plant, vehicles)	%
+	Current assets (e.g. stocks, debtors, bank and cash)	%
=	Total Assets	100 %

Finance (Liabilities)

	Capital (Shareholders' capital and reserves)	%
+	Provisions (for liabilities and charges)	%
+	Long-term debt (with currencies exceeding one year)	%
+	Current liabilities (Creditors, bank, etc.)	%
=	Total capital employed	100 %

Panel 12

Comparative financial analysis is an important tool of risk assessment. Especially in cases where authoritative data is not available, a bank is likely to use its own database for the purpose, that is, the financial statements of its clients. Irrespective of whether or not you can draw on relevant external sources of information, it remains necessary for you to be prepared for this peer group analysis. If needs be, you have to trust your own experience and knowledge of your industry to draw up, as objectively as you can, the 'ideal' cost and financial structure of a company in that industry.

Environmental influences on supply conditions

Some of these influences may already have been considered in the special context of industry attractiveness. However, the difference in viewpoints notwithstanding, the potential sources of external influences are essentially the same for markets as for industries. For your convenience, the selection included earlier in the context of market analysis is repeated here.

Environmental influences

Economy
for example:
- ☐ Economic growth and business cycle
- ☐ Balance of payments and currency rates
- ☐ Employment/unemployment
- ☐ Financial markets and interest rates

Technology
for example:
- ☐ Mature technologies
- ☐ New technologies
- ☐ Relevant life cycles

Government
for example:
- ☐ Legislation
- ☐ Economic and financial policies
- ☐ Taxation
- ☐ Subsidies

Demography
for example:
- ☐ Age pyramid
- ☐ Income groups
- ☐ Household/family units
- ☐ Geographic distribution

Culture
for example:
- ☐ Life style
- ☐ Fashion
- ☐ Public opinion

Panel 13

STRENGTHS AND STRATEGIES OF COMPETITORS

When speaking of your competitors it is assumed that included among them are suppliers of products that can be used as substitutes or offer alternative means of satisfying the customer needs your product addresses. Competitor analysis has two major dimensions:

1   The conditions which determine the intensity and aggressiveness of competition in your industry.
2   The competitive strengths and weaknesses of major competitors or groups of competitors distinguishable by criteria of competitive relevance.

Competitive conditions

Competition among the members of an industry is usually discussed under these three headings:

Competitive conditions

Structural factors

for example:
- ☐ Intensity of price competition
- ☐ Monopolistic or oligopolistic features of competition
- ☐ Cartels and other restrictions of competition
- ☐ Restriction of competition by regulations and public policy

Exit barriers

for example:
- ☐ High level of specialised investment in plant
- ☐ High level of staff specialisation
- ☐ Integration with other business units in a chain of backward or forward linkages
- ☐ Tradition and owner/management preferences

Threat of new competition

for example:
- ☐ Entry barriers to potential newcomers
- ☐ Emergence of substitute products
- ☐ Tendency of demand switching to substitutes

Panel 14

Competitor strengths and weaknesses

You will probably know the identity of your competitors, at least those that pose a major and immediate threat. Most likely you will find it more difficult, however, to identify individual strategies. Even so, your experience and knowledge of your industry will enable you to recognise certain distinctive approaches to market strategy in your competitive environment. You will also be aware of prominent strategic strengths and weaknesses among your competitors.

If the number of competitors is too large to deal with each individually, a pragmatic solution is to group them by distinctive criteria, such as the following:

Dividing competitors into strategic groups

Possible criteria

for example:
- ☐ Market share, price leadership
- ☐ Visibility, advertising activity
- ☐ Low price, mass production
- ☐ Customer service orientation
- ☐ Product differentiation, serving several market segments
- ☐ Organisation of distribution channel, forward linkages
- ☐ Organisation of supply, backward linkages
- ☐ State of production technology
- ☐ Products serving several uses
- ☐ Substitute products

Panel 15

Having assembled the strategic profiles which specify the competitive challenge confronting you, we can proceed to an assessment of the degree to which your competitors, individually and/or as members of a strategic group, fulfil the success conditions for suppliers we have identified earlier.

Fulfilment of critical success conditions by your firm and its competitors

Example case

Success factors[1]	Weights (Sum =100) [1]	Fulfilment rates (%)					
		Your firm [2]	Competitors				
			A	B	C	D	E
Market share:	*14*		*34*	*18*	*15*	*11*	*8*
1. Demand orientation	15	80	60	90	80	70	40
2. Visibility in the target market	14	40	70	60	30	40	80
3. Trade finance for customers	12	60	80	60	70	30	50
4. Delivery terms	10	50	50	60	40	50	50
5. Quality standards	10	90	70	90	60	50	70
6. Reliability of suppliers	9	70	40	50	50	30	50
7. Prices of raw materials	9	30	50	40	50	50	40
8. Marketing support for distributors	6	50	70	80	20	30	40
9. Distributor indemnification	6	70	50	-	40	-	-
10. Brand and corporate image	5	20	70	90	80	30	60
11. Product technology	4	70	50	70	60	40	50

1 see Table 1 on page 55
2 see Table 2 on page 57

Table 3

The tabulated data can be processed to obtain a ranking of suppliers to your target market, including your own enterprise, in terms of relative competitive strength, as shown in the following table.

Comparison of competitive strengths between your firm and its competitors

Example case

Success factors[1]	Weights (Sum =100)[1]	Index of competitive strength = Weight x Fulfilment rate / 100 [3]					
		Your firm[2]	Competitors				
			A	B	C	D	E
Market share:	*14*		*34*	*18*	*15*	*11*	*8*
1. Demand orientation	15	12.0	9.0	13.5	12.0	10.5	6.0
2. Visibility in the target market	14	5.6	9.8	8.4	4.2	5.6	11.2
3. Trade finance for customers	12	7.2	9.6	7.2	8.4	3.6	6.0
4. Delivery terms	10	5.0	5.0	6.0	4.0	5.0	5.0
5. Quality standards	10	9.0	7.0	9.0	6.0	5.0	7.0
6. Reliability of suppliers	9	6.3	3.6	4.5	4.5	2.7	4.5
7. Prices of raw materials	9	2.7	4.5	3.6	4.5	4.5	3.6
8. Marketing support for distributors	6	3.0	4.2	4.8	1.2	1.8	2.4
9. Distributor indemnification	6	4.2	3.0	0.0	2.4	0.0	0.0
10. Brand and corporate image	5	1.0	3.5	4.5	4.0	1.5	3.0
11. Product technology	4	2.8	2.0	2.8	2.4	1.6	2.0
Summary index of competitive strength:		58.8	61.2	64.3	53.6	41.8	50.7
Ranking by competitive strength:		3	2	1	4	6	5

1 see Table 1 on page 55
2 see Table 2 on page 57
3 see Table 3 on page 64

Table 4

THE RELATIVE COMPETITIVE STRENGTH OF YOUR FIRM

We have now reached the stage where we can evaluate your relative competitive strength, that is, the fundamental condition determining the success potential and risk of your enterprise.

The comparison of index numbers in the above table indicates the difference in competitive strength between any two members of the strategic group and, specifically, between your enterprise and any of its competitors.

There is a possible qualification you might consider at this point: certain differences in competitive strength between the units or groups shown up in the comparison may have other causes than the capacity for fulfilling the relevant success conditions. For the purposes of our analysis we have implicitly treated each competitor as a strategic business unit under its own management, with access to finance depending on its own prospects.

In certain cases this may not be realistic, especially if a unit is affiliated to or integrated in a larger and more powerful organisation, private or public. The effect on the unit's competitive strength can be considerable. There may be backing or support in terms of management, operations and finance. There may also be disadvantages such as overriding constraints of policy, direct interference with management, operational inflexibility due to linkages with other units, and the allotment of finance according to higher level strategies.

The result could be an overall strengthening or weakening of the unit's competitive position. In such cases you might wish to adjust the relevant column of index figures in Table 4 by multiplication with a factor representing your estimation of the likely effect.

Comparing strengths with your peer group

When comparing the competitive strength of your enterprise with that of your competitors in respect of individual success conditions you may find that relative weaknesses in one category are compensated by relative strengths in others. For obtaining overall measures of strengths and weaknesses to guide your strategic planning, we need to combine the various competing units and groups (marked A to E in our example) in one group of competitors.

The relative competitive strength of your firm

Example case

Success factors	Comparative index *		Relative strengths and weaknesses of your enterprise
	Your firm	Your competitors	
1. Demand orientation	12.0	10.4	+1.6 = +15.4 %
2. Visibility in the target market	5.6	8.1	-2.5 = -30.9 %
3. Trade finance for customers	7.2	7.8	-0.6 = -7.7 %
4. Delivery terms	5.0	5.0	0 = 0 %
5. Quality standards	9.0	7.0	+2.0 = +28.6 %
6. Reliability of suppliers	6.3	3.9	+2.4 = +61.5 %
7. Prices of raw materials	2.7	4.2	-1.5 = -35.7 %
8. Marketing support for	3.0	3.3	-0.3 = -9.1 %
9. Distributor indemnification	4.2	1.6	+2.6 =+162.5 %
10. Brand and corporate image	1.0	3.5	-2.5 = -71.4 %
11. Product technology	2.8	2.2	+0.6 = +27.3 %
Summary result:	58.8	57.0	+1.8 = +3.2 %

* see Table 4 on page 66

Table 5

In order to obtain meaningful measures of competitive strength for the group as a whole it is necessary to differentiate the contributions of its members by suitable weight parameters. In most cases the appropriate criterion will be market share. The adjustment is accomplished by applying your estimates of market share (such as those included in Tables 3 and 4) as factors (percentages divided by the total share of the group, that is 100 minus your market share, in our example: 100 – 14 = 86) to the relevant columns in Table 4. Table 5 below shows the result obtained for the example data.

A caveat regarding ranking arithmetic

The procedure has been kept deliberately simple. The calculations are easily performed on a spreadsheet, for instance with Microsoft Excel. When interpreting the results, it is necessary, however, to be aware of the limitations of arithmetic in this context.

You have seen that the inputs are, by their nature, mostly qualitative judgements. These we have attempted to quantify by methods of rating and ranking. For all your endeavour at detached objectivity such methods will always be fraught with a considerable subjective element. Obviously, the statistical treatment of such inputs cannot produce an exactness that is not inherent in them, especially not a digital exactness.

Consequently, the results are useable only in the dimensions of the source data, that is, strictly only as indicators of order in rating or ranking sequences.

Assessing your competitive strengths and weaknesses

With the last step of the analysis illustrated in Table 5 above you have obtained a profile of competitive strengths and weaknesses on which to orient your strategic action plan.

For drawing such conclusion it is, of course, necessary to identify the reasons for the most significant differences in competitive potential which stand out in the analysis. As was emphasised before:

> Experience shows that an enterprise achieves enduring success mainly on a solid foundation of sustainable competitive advantage.

Therefore, a question prominent in a rater's mind will be whether the competitive advantages identified by your analysis are, in fact, sustainable and for how long.

Another question is whether the apparent competitive weaknesses in certain categories are wholly or partly compensated by strengths in others. A related question is, of course, whether there remains a net advantage favouring your enterprise over its competitors. The point has been made that the arithmetical results of ranking methods can only be interpreted as broad indications of an order. This means that they are useful in establishing relative weaknesses and strengths, but that the numerical magnitude of such differences needs to be interpreted with great caution.

Such caution is indicated, in particular, when considering the capacity for mutual compensation between two conditions of an essentially different kind. For instance, in our example the most apparent 'competitive gaps' exist regarding the success conditions (10) 'Brand and corporate image', (7) 'Prices of raw materials' and (2) 'Visibility in the target market'. Arithmetically, one single advantage, namely the one regarding condition (9) 'Distributor indemnification', would suffice to compensate all these deficits. It may be doubted, though, whether, in reality, an advantage in that particular category would substantially mitigate the recognised weaknesses.

In order to place our rating exercise in proper perspective: arithmetical analysis has an auxiliary function. It makes your argumentation more pointed and succinct, but it does not obviate the need of defending your underlying assumptions. Yet the systematic method has the potential of significantly enhancing the credibility of your analysis, because it lends to it a degree of objectivity which is distinctly superior to a mere voicing of opinions.

In creating this semblance of objectivity one essential prerequisite is honesty, especially honesty with yourself. Obviously, it makes no sense to cheat at solitaire. But it is equally obvious that subjectivity in self-analysis can never be fully eliminated, not even in its particularly insidious form of wishful thinking. The method of obtaining a measure of relative competitive strength outlined above endeavours to minimise subjectivity by building on a diverse set of contributing elements each of which is considered separately. Thereby the impact of the individual element on the overall result is rendered less obvious and, thus, the scope for reflexive subconscious interference reduced. The effect is considerably enhanced, where the contributing elements are supplied by different sources or persons. Another factor helping to confuse the subjective reflex is that competitive strength is defined not in absolute but in relative terms.

One effective way of 'alienating' the analytical process is having all or parts of it performed by external advisors. Care needs to be taken, though, that management remains closely involved. As pointed out earlier: plans must be made by the people responsible for their implementation in order to convince third parties. An over-reliance on outside opinion may raise doubts about your managerial competence.

However, the most effective safeguard against the pitfalls of subjectivity is one of attitude:

Recognising strategic weaknesses is a competitive advantage, ignoring them a serious handicap.

The rational way to deal with strategic weaknesses is to weigh, in terms of feasibility and costs, the options of reducing or removing them against those of building or reinforcing compensatory strategic strengths.

Needless to say, the results of self-rating ought to be used with circumspection. For it to have the desired effect, the addressed party should have no difficulty appreciating its method for what it is and follow its logic. This is the reason for the simplicity of the approach demonstrated. In my experience, attempts at methodical sophistication over and above the requirements of the practical context are not merely a waste of effort, but may well prove counterproductive. In any case, in the majority of occasions there will be no call for presenting the actual analysis in any detail. It is meant, in the first instance, to arm you with a well-founded confidence in the case you present to your raters.

11 *Strategic Consequences*

Having built your case along the lines of the preceding chapters you are now in a position to present the principles of your strategy, especially its main thrust and the measures of its implementation, with the clarity and conciseness of a 'Mission Statement'. More to the point, you are now ready to specify your financial requirements in terms of type, amount and timing. Your financial plan carries little conviction unless shown to derive cogently from a well reasoned strategy.

The importance of competitive advantages has already been emphasised. Building a capacity for satisfying customer demand is mainly a matter of competence and means. An adequate supply efficiency, as such, can usually be obtained with a high degree of certainty. Far more uncertain is a firm's ability to prevail against competitors and correspondingly high the risk of its failure for lack of competitive strength. Therefore, the central principle of strategic planning is gaining, and maintaining, competitive advantage.

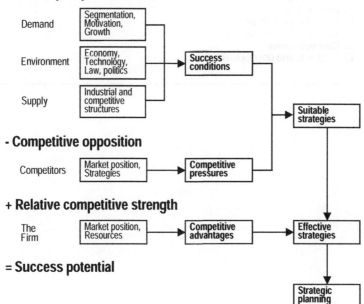

Competitive Advantage
the central principle of strategic planning

Success prospects of the market

Demand	Segmentation, Motivation, Growth
Environment	Economy, Technology, Law, politics
Supply	Industrial and competitive structures

Success conditions

- Competitive opposition

| Competitors | Market position, Strategies |

Competitive pressures

+ Relative competitive strength

| The Firm | Market position, Resources |

Competitive advantages

Suitable strategies

Effective strategies

Strategic planning

= Success potential

Figure 4

The formulation of your strategic plan requires three steps:

Step one — Specification of your corporate mission in terms of the principles and goals that will guide your strategic actions.

Step two — Specification of the major thrusts of your strategy, that is, the currently most important strategic goals and the directions in which they are to be pursued.

Step three — Specification of the measures required to attain those goals and a time-critical plan of implementing them.

Goals of corporate policy

By definition, a strategy is goal oriented. Obviously, most enterprises are in business for a financial result, usually expressed as return on investment. But there are other policy goals which affect the specifics of a strategy as guiding principles.

Policy goals

Long-term
for example:
☐ Market segmentation
☐ Diversification
☐ Standards of product quality
☐ Staff welfare
☐ International expansion

Near-term
for example:
☐ New markets
☐ Market share
☐ Financial consolidation
☐ Takeovers and affiliations
☐ Cost economies
☐ Research and development

Panel 16

The corporate mission

The strategic mission of an enterprise is defined by the identified success factors to be translated into strategic action. It has typically these dimensions:

Dimensions of the corporate mission

Customer needs addressed
for example:
☐ Unmet customer needs
☐ Means of buyer motivation
☐ Preferred ordering channels

Product attributes
for example:
☐ Degree of need orientation
☐ Features enhancing customer appeal
☐ Unique/innovative attributes

Target markets
for example:
☐ Target groups of customers
☐ Demand size and growth
☐ Sales/market share potential

Essential operational technologies
for example:
☐ Upgrading to new technology standards
☐ Own research and development
☐ Required investments

Synergetic linkages
for example:
☐ Kinds of linkage considered
☐ Means and strategies of obtaining these
☐ Investments required

Distinctive competences and resources
for example:
☐ Staff
☐ Research
☐ Patented product technology

Panel 17

Strategic thrusts

Business strategy pursues two major goals corresponding with the two root sources of business success (compare Figure 2 on page 34):

1 Sales growth deriving from the capacity to satisfy customer needs.
2 Market position deriving from the ability to withstand competition.

If our analysis is applied at the level of a company controlling several subsidiaries, a third consideration of strategic thrust enters here:

3   Portfolio policy aiming to coordinate and optimise the set of subsidiary strategies.

GROWTH STRATEGY

The classic market-product matrix suggests four major strategic directions in which to pursue sales growth. A second dimension of a growth strategy is the creation of new scope for growth.

Main thrusts of growth strategy

The classic growth vectors

- ☐ Deeper market penetration (present markets, present products)
- ☐ Broader product range (present markets, new products)
- ☐ Expanding market scope (new markets, present products)
- ☐ Diversification (new markets, new products)

Creating scope for growth

for example:
- ☐ New distinctive technologies
- ☐ New distinctive competences
- ☐ Backward and forward linkages
- ☐ Horizontal integration

Panel 18

COMPETITIVE STRATEGY

An enterprise has basically three weapons with which to fortify and expand its market position against competitors:

1 **Differentiation** – Making one's products better than those of one's competitors or, at least, different. This is the most frequently employed strategy.
2 **Low price** – A low price strategy needs to be solidly founded on cost advantages to succeed. Price competition is considered as the most dangerous competitive strategy, since it can easily trigger price wars with often ruinous consequences for the weaker party.
3 **Specialisation** – This is the strategy of market segmentation which has generally proved the most successful of the three strategies.

Main thrusts of competitive strategy

Product differentiation

for example:
☐ Design
☐ Quality
☐ Functionality
☐ Patent protection
☐ Innovative attributes
☐ Customer service
☐ Mode of distribution
☐ Brand image

Low price

for example:
☐ Production economies
☐ Vertical integration
☐ Cheap raw materials
☐ Low staff costs
☐ Subsidies
☐ Advantages of location

Specialisation

for example:
☐ Niche markets
☐ Narrow product range
☐ Geographic focus
☐ Specialised research

Panel 19

STRATEGIC INVESTMENTS

If your enterprise controls subsidiaries which have the status of strategic business units, you will have a strategy for each. But these will be subsumed under an over-arching group strategy. That circumstance gains relevance, when considering the allocation of funds from a common pool among the members of the group. The strategic options are summarised in the matrix that follows.

Basic investment strategies

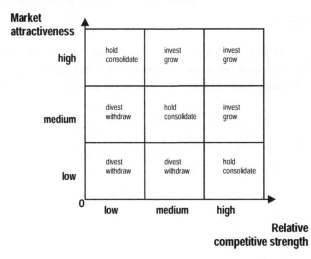

Figure 5

Your plan of strategic action

A plan of strategic action is drawn up in three steps:

Step one   Define the scope for actively promoting the success of your business.
Step two   Identify the key result areas where effective action can be expected strongly to enhance the performance of your enterprise.
Step three Assess your ability to act effectively in the identified result areas in terms of a strengths and weaknesses analysis.

THE SCOPE FOR STRATEGIC ACTION

In planning strategic action your first step is the identification of the major areas in which action can be expected to be most effective. They are conveniently defined in terms of operational sectors as summarised below.

The major domains of strategic action

1. Income generation
   (Primary strategies)
   1.1 Marketing and distribution
   1.2 Products and product development
   1.3 Operational organisation and processes

2. Resources
   (Secondary strategies)
   2.1 Production
   2.2 Supplies
   2.3 Personnel
   2.4 Finance

Panel 20

KEY RESULT AREAS

Within the broad areas of strategic scope which you consider most suitable for strategic action we need to identify the key result areas that are specifically relevant for your strategy.

Here follows a selection of examples of such result areas in each of the major domains of strategic action.

Key result areas of strategic action

1. Income generation

(Primary strategies)

1.1 Marketing and Distribution

for example:
- ☐ Marketing concept and sales plan
- ☐ Relevant market information
- ☐ Market segmentation/specialisation
- ☐ Product differentiation
- ☐ Breadth of product range
- ☐ Closeness of customer relations
- ☐ Extensive customer service
- ☐ Brand image development
- ☐ Distributive efficiency
- ☐ Advertising and public relations
- ☐ Pricing

1.2 Products and product development

for example:
- ☐ Need-oriented production program
- ☐ Technical competence
- ☐ Research and development capacity
- ☐ Access to innovative technologies

1.3 Operational organisation and processes

for example:
- ☐ Size of operations
- ☐ Geographical location
- ☐ Functional coordination
- ☐ Integration of processes
- ☐ Production planning
- ☐ Stock management
- ☐ Ordering and billing systems
- ☐ Bookkeeping
- ☐ Financial controlling

2. Resources

(Secondary strategies)

2.1 Production

for example:
- ☐ Output capacity
- ☐ Plant technology
- ☐ Production know-how
- ☐ Organisation of production processes
- ☐ Cost efficiency

2.2 Supplies

for example:
- ☐ Supplier loyalty
- ☐ Supply efficiency
- ☐ Prices
- ☐ Trade finance
- ☐ Backward linkages

2.3 Personnel

for example:
- ☐ Functional qualification
- ☐ Specialist competence
- ☐ Salary levels
- ☐ Staff motivation
- ☐ Training schemes
- ☐ Staff productivity

2.4 Finance

for example:
- ☐ Cash generating capacity
- ☐ Extent of current banking facilities
- ☐ Access to finance for productive investments
- ☐ Access to sources of equity funds

Panel 21

RATING STRATEGIC STRENGTHS AND WEAKNESSES

You will notice that our frame of reference has shifted. In the preceding chapters we have been preoccupied with the success conditions of your markets and your competitive strength in terms of your present ability to meet these conditions. Now we are looking at the ways and means by which, given the requisite finance, you expect to increase your success potential in both directions.

These ways and means are now to be assessed in terms of the key result areas you have defined along the lines of the above panel as well as the practical and financial feasibility of realising them.

For the purposes of illustration two domains of strategic action have been selected from the panel and your expected ability of effective action in the relevant result areas rated in percentage terms.

It remains for you to decide in which strategic domain and in which result area or areas to take action in order to eliminate a strategic weakness or enhance a strategic strength. Naturally, the focus of such considerations is on weaknesses that constitute, or might turn into, serious competitive threats. These prominent weaknesses are often referred to as 'strategic gaps'.

The strategic strength of your firm in key result areas

Example case

Strategic domain: 1.2 Products and product development	
Key result areas	Efficiency rating
Need-oriented production program	80 %
Technical competence	70 %
Research and development capacity	20 %
Access to innovative technologies	30 %

Strategic domain: 2.2 Supplies	
Key result areas	Efficiency rating
Supplier loyalty	80 %
Supply efficiency	30 %
Prices	70 %
Backward linkages	10 %

Table 6

YOUR REQUIREMENT OF RESOURCES AND ACTION PLAN

Closing strategic gaps requires the expenditure of resources. Often enough a recognised gap will be difficult or even impossible to close for practical or technical reasons. More frequently, however, the limiting factor is the availability of finance.

Strategic gaps
and typical measures taken to close them

Product gap
    Identify new user applications for the product
    Add new attributes to enhance appeal and usefulness

Distribution gap
    Increase the density of market coverage
    Expand the distribution network

Production gap
    Expand output capacity
    Expand the product range

Supply gap
    Find more economic materials
    Find more efficient suppliers

Competitive gap
    Win market share from competitors
    Win market share from suppliers of substitute products

Demand gap
    Improve the effectiveness of marketing efforts
    Enter new markets

Panel 22

We have now arrived at the stage where you can begin to think of your strategy not merely as a statement of broad intentions, but in the specific terms of individual tasks to be carried out.

The translation of your strategy into a plan of action in directly executable terms is a vital step without which your planning effort will remain an abstract scheme without practical relevance.

Unless you have specified the required action, you will not be able to specify the resources required, in each instance, to enable such action.

Unless you have specified your requirement of resources you will not be able to specify the finance required to obtain them.

The following is an example of how the practical implications of your action plan, including the financial ones, can be summarised:

Plan of strategic action by strategic domain and key result area
Example case

Strategic domain: 1.2 Products and product development

Plan year: 1

Result areas	Target Efficiency rating up from → to	Measures to be implemented	Finance required			Reference to related domains
			Current costs p.m.	Investment/ expenditure	Month in plan year	
1. Need-oriented production program	80→90%	Expand range Z by two product types		10 000	1	1.3
		Production planning				
		Product type A:		275 000	2	
		Plant X1		325 000	4	
		Plant X2		130 000	1	
		Related equipment X1, X2	4 000		from 1	2.3
		Operating staff:	4 000		from 3	
		for X1				
		for X2	2 700		from 6	
		Product type B:		27 000	5	
		Plant X3 (leased)	3 500		from 5	2.3
		Related equipment X3				
		Operating staff for X3				
2. Technical competence	70→90%	Employ qualified engineer with experience in operating type X plant as assistant production manager	10 000		from 1	2.3
3. Research and development	20→60%	Extensions to R&D laboratory				1.3 2.3
		Additional staff:	12 000		from 7	
		Chemist (department head)	4 000		from 7	
		Assistant 1	3 500		from 9	
		Assistant 2		45 000	6	
		Furniture and fittings	6 500		from 7	
		Scientific equipment (leased)				
4. Access to innovative technologies	30→70%	Participation in research project at University M	5 000		from 4	

Table 7

The final step in planning your strategic action is the coordination of the individual measures in terms of time. In our sample case the timing schedule might look like this:

Time plan for strategic action
(Plan year 1)

Example case

Strategic domain /result area	Measures	1	2	3	4	5	6	7	8	9	10	11	12
1.2 / 2	Engineer (asst. prod. manager)	□											
1.2 / 1	Operating staff for X1	□	□										
1.2 / 1	Production planning	□	□	□									
1.2 / 1	Related equipment X1/X2	□	□										
1.2 / 1	Plant X1			□	□								
1.2 / 1	Operating staff for X2				□	□							
1.2 / 1	Plant X2					□	□						
1.2 / 4	Research project University M					□	□	□	□				
1.2 / 1	Related equipment X3						□	□					
1.2 / 1	Operating staff for X3						□						
1.2 / 1	Plant X3 (lease)							□	□				
1.2 / 2	Lab furniture and fittings							□	□	□			
1.2 / 2	Scientific equipment (lease)								□	□			
1.2 / 2	Chemist (dept. head)								□				
1.2 / 2	Lab assistant 1								□				
1.2 / 2	Lab assistant 2										□		

Table 8

Summary of the task accomplished

The purpose of this book is to equip you with a method of preparing your enterprise and yourself for the vicissitudes of a credit rating which decides your access to finance. In view of the importance of the outcome we had to be thorough in raising the issues that might be expected to have a bearing on the process.

One function of the book is to serve you as a checklist of issues potentially relevant to a rating test. It is impossible, of course, for such a list to be exhaustive in the literal sense. What the book aims to achieve, though, is, first, to expose the concepts underlying all rating methods as a coherent system of straightforward logic and, second, provide the tools by which to put them to practical use.

It is hoped that our discussion has left you in no doubt that your financing project cannot be convincingly argued without a solid foundation of strategic reasoning from which it derives by a logic that is readily conclusive also from the viewpoint of an outsider.

Where we stand, we have achieved three important intermediate goals:

- A conclusive argument of your prospects of success.
- A concise description of your strategy.
- A convincing derivation of your financial requirements.

In order to quantify our conclusions we have taken your enterprise through a two-stage rating process. First, we have obtained a rating in terms of the success conditions of your market with the result shown in Table 1 (page 55). Next we have placed that result in an industry perspective and arrived at a measure of your competitive strength as per Table 5 (page 57). Substantially, the inputs to the process derive from your knowledge of the two sets of conditions which provide the decisive benchmarks: firstly, your market and your target customer group and, secondly, your industry and your competitors. Thus, the rating process is, at the same time, a telling test of your management competence which after all is the foundation of your bankers' confidence.

Our next major task is to quantify the implications of your strategy in financial terms. Your bankers will expect you to present a projection of financial statements meeting accepted reporting standards and extending to a time horizon that includes the term of the financial support you are seeking.

PART III

Passing the Test: Step Two – Drawing the Financial Conclusions

12 *The Task Outlined*

Your banker or investor expects your financial plan to be easy to absorb, yet detailed enough to be conclusive. Its basic format is no problem. It follows general conventions of accounting. An all too often neglected problem, though, is the physical presentation. It is supposed to enable the comparison of data across a number of planning periods on severely limited page space. Effective communication being a key factor in 'selling' your project, layout is no minor issue.

By nature of their occupation, you will expect your bankers and their credit raters to be competent financial analysts and especially demanding in this respect. Their methods are no different from those of the 'fundamental analysis' applied by stock exchange analysts to the financial statements of listed companies. There is an important difference though: the data available to the fundamental analyst is mostly limited to what can be gleaned from a company's annual reports, the latest of which is often many months out of date at the time of publication. By contrast, your banker is able to insist on information that is current, and he or she can ask for additional detail wherever an item seems deserving of closer attention.

The banker, however, has a limiting problem, too, and a very serious one: he or she can, in the normal course of business, spend only so much time and effort on an individual case. And there is not only the initial rating of new customers to perform, but also the periodical re-rating of all exposures as stipulated by Basel II (see quote on page 28 *(425)*).

A considerable amount of academic research has been invested in finding a way out of this practical impasse, and the findings suggest that a pragmatic solution exists: certain indicators composed of financial statement data have been shown, within statistical confidence intervals, to have predictive power regarding the incidence of customer default. This also seems to mitigate the problem of financial statements being notoriously out of date. Later on we shall use one of the most popular methods to apply to your own data as a quick rating test.

It must not be forgotten, however, that the rating method is one of statistical probability applied to a large data universe. The confidence interval of such probabilities constitutes an ample margin for misjudging the individual case. This may be acceptable for a bank with a large portfolio. It can hardly be considered as fair, though, from your, the individual customer's, point of view.

Your only chance of escaping from the gamble of rating by averages is to demonstrate to your raters the individual probabilities that apply to *your* business. The technique by which to do that is dynamic financial planning.

Feeding your financial controlling system

Dynamic financial planning is also the foundation of financial controlling which your raters will want to see functioning smoothly in your administration. Specifically, it supplies the instruments on your controlling 'dashboard' with the current data needed for sensitive monitoring. Financial controlling means running a business by numbers, and the jargon terms 'controlling dashboard' and 'controlling cockpit' are particularly apt metaphors of its practical relevance to management.

In the following, therefore, we shall not merely discuss methods of financial analysis as might be applied by your raters. You will be provided with the tools for building, with a minimum of effort, an effective controlling 'cockpit' of your own. The worked example we shall be using to illustrate the process contains about 40 profit and loss account and balance sheet items. Intended to show the maximum requirement, that number somewhat overstates the requirement of any practical case. Adapting the template to your particular set of accounts by criteria of significance you are most likely to reduce the number to somewhere between 20 and 30 and you will definitely not require the number of worksheets (labelled Plansheets) included on pages 108 to 159 for the purpose of step-by-step illustration.

In our present context the aim is for simplicity as well as significance. You will not want to overload the raters' work programme. If anything, you want to make their job easier. Not the least consideration, of course, is to make your controlling cockpit easy to maintain on a high level of actuality. There is no point in overloading your dashboard either. With increasing complexity the marginal gains of sensitivity and significance tend to decrease rapidly.

Another practical reason for simplicity ought not to be underrated: the cost of time and effort to be invested in establishing an effective controlling system. Given the access to your company's accounts on a fairly high level of aggregation, you will be able to set up the system detailed below virtually single-handed, with no more help than a spreadsheet calculator such as Microsoft Excel. And you will find it easy to keep the system truly dynamic by feeding it the required input data at suitably frequent, such as monthly, intervals.

If you are in charge of financial controlling in a larger company you may have sophisticated and complex systems installed to do the data processing for you. Even you, however, might value a private 'pocket edition' that keeps the salient features and tendencies of your company's finances continually at your fingertips. This may suit you even more, if you are an executive who is not routinely concerned with the overall financial situation of the company, but wants to have a considered personal view of it at all times.

Awareness of the company's financial situation and all its implications is generally held to be a decisive criterion by which to judge the quality of its management and the personal competence of its executives. In communications with your bankers it is important to project that current awareness and be able, at any time, to present a reasoned assessment of the financial state of your business and its future development.

Even if you know all about financial analysis, you may find it instructive to check your understanding of a professional credit rater's preferred approach by scanning the exposition that follows.

The format of financial reporting

You are, of course, familiar with financial statements. If your enterprise is a going concern, your accounting system produces them regularly, at least annually, if only to satisfy commercial and tax laws. Invariably, your bankers will ask for the latest one. Even your latest statement, however, is about the past and your bankers and, hence, your raters, are really only interested in the future. To be specific, they want to be assured of your future ability to pay interest and principal on your debt and/or produce an adequate return on your equity, depending on the kind of their commitment. They will, therefore, insist on projections of income and cash flow over the period of their exposure, in the case of long-term debt or equity investment usually over a period of five years.

As emphasised before, your financial plan will be perceived as the quantification of your strategy in terms of currency. Given that the strategic constraints are essentially financial, it is a feasibility test of your strategy conditioned by the assumptions of adequate funding made in your plan.

Fortunately, the basic format of a financial plan presents no problem. To make it easy to peruse for any professional reader our exposition will follow the conventional format of financial reporting consisting of two major statements, the income statement (or profit and loss account) comparing revenue with expenditure and the balance sheet comparing assets and liabilities. These statements are prepared over convenient intervals such as months or years. Structure and detail of the projected statements will be such as to make their context with your strategy apparent. The data, however, will be of the same kind as that conventionally processed through your bookkeeping system. For the practical purposes of financial controlling it is, in any case, essential for financial accounting and planning systems to be perfectly compatible.

From bookkeeping to financial analysis

Your raters will subject your projected financial statements to an analysis similar to, if more thorough, than that applied by stock exchange analysts to the annual reports of listed companies. Your raters' analysis is focused on indicators of your PD, your 'Probability of Default'. In their conclusions they are guided by empirical studies carried out over lengthy periods. As described in the introductory chapters, banks opting for IRB, the 'Internal Rating Based Approach', will make use, especially, of their own statistically evidenced experience. We shall return to the methods of risk analysis and risk control later on. At this stage we are concerned with preparing the database from which those methods can draw meaningful conclusions.

In the final analysis, what bankers and raters are most interested in is your projection of cash flow and liquid reserves. It is important, therefore, that the financial plan is structured in such a manner that the projected movements of funds through the enterprise are sufficiently transparent.

The concepts of cash flow and liquidity are related but not identical. For interpreting and analysing financial statements it is important to distinguish between the two dimensions which are the basic structural elements of every modern accounting system, the dimensions of 'flow' and 'stock'.

Figure 6 illustrates the concepts.

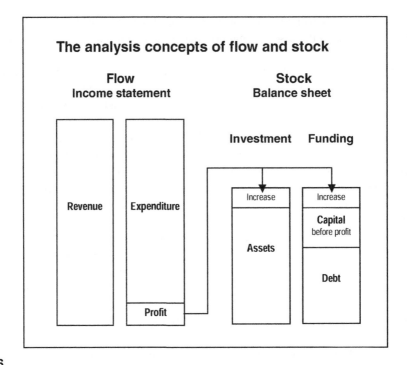

Figure 6

Degrees of transparency

Presenting a financial plan is a matter of balancing the demand for transparency with that of significance. Transparency in financial reporting is a recurring topic of professional and political debate. The consensus is reflected in generally accepted or legally enforced accounting principles. For bankers and raters transparency in financial statements is the first criterion by which to rate management quality.

On the other hand, too much detail can be counterproductive. One way of striking an acceptable compromise is to organise the presentation of the data on several levels of disaggregation from a two-page summary of consolidated income statement and balance sheet data downwards. Experience shows that the 'readability' of financial plans is an important factor in creating confidence and acceptance. This is why in the following discussion of financial planning principles the treatment of data content and analysis methods will be closely aligned to this practical requirement.

13 *Accounts: The Conventional Framework*

There are well-established international standards of financial analysis and financial planning, and you will wish to make sure that your financial plan meets those standards. Your plan will be expected to describe the past, present and future of your enterprise in terms of currency. This chapter outlines a systematic framework for the task. Its arithmetic puts numbers to your profit potential. It also tells you and your funders what amounts of finance in which categories will be needed to realise it.

Elementary analysis

The first level of financial analysis presents no methodical problem. Analysing a company's accounts under the heads of income statement and balance sheet is common practice throughout the business world. It involves no more than a systematic aggregation of bookkeeping or planning data into meaningful summaries.

Financial analysis
The first level

Income statement
typical subjects:
- ☐ Sources of income
- ☐ Direct costs of income generation
- ☐ Major categories of administrative costs
- ☐ Cost of finance
- ☐ Extraneous income and expenditure
- ☐ Profit for shareholders

Balance sheet
Assets (Investment)
typical subjects:
- ☐ Long-term and fixed investments
- ☐ Provisions for depreciation
- ☐ Self-liquidating investments
- ☐ Cash and other liquidity reserves

Liabilities (Funding)
typical subjects:
- ☐ Shareholders' capital and reserves
- ☐ Provisions for future obligations and contingencies
- ☐ Long-term debt
- ☐ Current debt

Panel 23

Focused analysis

The second level of analysis processes the data compiled on the first level in order to arrive at conclusions as to your continued financial health, specifically, the risk of providing the requested finance. In as much as all financial statements are structured on the same basic principles, certain methods of financial analysis, too, have tended to become standardised.

Financial analysis
The second level

Financial structure
Assets and liabilities expressed as percentages of the
balance sheet total

> typical applications:
> ☐ Comparing financing periods with asset life
> ☐ Testing the relative sufficiency of own means
> ☐ Comparisons with industry or peer group averages

Cash flow
Analysis of the inflows and outflows of cash during
a period

> typical applications:
> ☐ Testing the self-financing capacity of the enterprise
> ☐ Testing the dependence on external short-term finance
> ☐ Tracing the causes of changes in liquidity

Liquid Reserves
Analysis of the means of payment and the current
claims on them

> typical applications:
> ☐ Establishing the firm's current state of solvency
> ☐ Tracing changes in the components of liquid reserves
> ☐ Assessing the sustainable level of liquid reserves

Panel 24

Ratio analysis, the third level of financial analysis, investigates the various interactions of the four major components of the financial statement: revenue, expenditure, assets and liabilities. Its methods belong to the standard equipment of the financial analyst. Ratio analysis is of special interest to our discussion because it is also the preferred tool of credit raters. Most scoring models developed by professional rating agencies are based on ratios.

Financial analysis
The third level

Rating Indicators
Ratio analysis testing significant relationships between
various items in balance sheet and income statement

Main areas of application:

☐ Equity gearing

☐ Indebtedness

☐ Liquidity

☐ Profitability

☐ Productivity

☐ Terms of trade

☐ Debt cover by cash flow

☐ Growth

Panel 25

A general framework for assessing financial risk

The following three listings outline a general framework of financial analysis which will in most practical cases answer the purposes of rating and meet both the principles of transparency and lucidity. The first two panels show the main heads under which to organise your database in the two dimensions of income statement and balance sheet, while the third structures the three major categories of processed data.

Main heads of financial analysis

I. Income and expenditure (income statement)

Sales revenue

- Rebates etc.
+ Adjustments (net)

= **Operating income**

- Variable costs

= **Gross operating profit**

- Depreciation of assets

- Staff costs

- General overheads

+ Other operating revenue
- Other operating costs

= **Net operating profit**

- Cost of finance (net)

+ Extraordinary revenue (net)

= **Net profit before tax**

- Taxation

= **Net profit after tax**

If warranted, broken down by product groups, market segments etc.

Capitalised value added by own work to plant and equipment, change in stock values, discounts granted, bonuses received etc.

Cost of sales, specifically cost of materials and components, external services etc.

If broken down by type or category, the detail to be compatible with that applied to depreciating fixed assets in the balance sheet.

Grouped according to operating unit and function. Required separately: a compatibly detailed schedule of numbers of staff employed.

Grouped according to operating unit and kind of expenditure.

Interest and similar charges payable and receivable by type of finance.

Panel 26

Main heads of financial analysis

II. Investment and funding (balance sheet)

Investment (assets)

Depreciating fixed assets:
   Tangible fixed assets
   Intangible fixed assets
      if warranted, broken down further by type or category
      (the breakdown to be compatible with that applied
      to provisions for depreciation in the income statement)
Investments in associated companies
Long-term financial investments
Other long-term assets

Fixed assets

Stocks, specifically:
   Work in progress and finished goods
   Raw materials
   Consumables
Working capital, specifically:
   Trade debtors
   Other current assets
   Cash and balances with banks

\+ **Current assets**

\= **Total investment**

Funding (liabilities)

Shareholders' capital
Shareholders' loans and investments
Profit and loss account, consisting of:
   Balance carried forward
   Profit/loss for the period

Shareholders' funds

Provisions (e.g. for tax liabilities, guarantees etc.)

Finance from associated companies
Long-term debt
Current liabilities, specifically:
   Trade creditors
   Other current liabilities
   Bank advances and overdrafts

\+ **Total debt**

\= **Total funding**

Panel 27

Main heads of financial analysis

Financial indicators

III. Financial structure

1. Income and expenditure
organised compatibly with income statement (I)

2. Investment and funding
organised compatibly with balance sheet (II)

IV. Cash flow and liquid reserves

Cash flow
1. Cash inflow from business activity
2. Actual use of cash for payments
3. Inflow of cash from funders
4. Disposable cash flow

Liquid reserves
5. Change in reserves
6. Composition of liquid reserves

V. Rating indicators

1. Equity gearing
2. Indebtedness
3. Liquidity
4. Profitability
5. Productivity
6. Terms of trade
7. Debt cover by cash flow
8. Growth

Panel 28

14 *Income and Liquidity: The Dual Focus of Analysts*

Lenders or investors have two overriding concerns: the ability of your business to yield an adequate return and the possibility of its failure which, technically, is a shortage of liquid funds. They will want to know how financial inputs and outputs in your company interact to produce the projected yields. But, since it takes liquidity to produce yields, they will be equally interested to see how you propose to sustain it at a sufficient level. Your plan will need to address both these concerns.

Focus number one: Income generation and return on investment

Investment in this context is defined as the total of all assets employed in your enterprise. This is the balance sheet total, that is, the totality of funds, own means as well as borrowings, invested in these assets. Somewhat ambiguously that total is also referred to as total capital employed.

The return on investment (ROI) is the sum of earnings before interest and tax (EBIT) during an accounting period (usually a year) accruing to the owners of the invested funds expressed as a percentage of total assets. Because the term investment may be used in other specific senses in a company's accounts, some analysts prefer to speak of the return on assets (ROA).

The return on investment accrues to two groups of funders: lenders have the first claim on it for interest (including interest type charges such as discounts on commercial paper etc.). The remainder, that is, the net profit, remunerates the firm's owners or shareholders for providing its capital base. (The corporate tax charged against it is, essentially, a tax on shareholders' income.)

$$\text{Return on investment} \ (\% \ \text{p.a.}) = \frac{\text{EBIT}}{\text{total assets}} \times 100$$

Return on investment can be shown to have two major components: return on sales and asset turnover. (A somewhat ambiguous alternative term used by analysts for asset turnover is capital turnover, where capital stands for total funds employed, hence, equals total assets.)

$$\text{Return on investment} \ (\% \ \text{p.a.}) = \text{return on sales} \times \text{asset turnover}$$

$$= \frac{\text{EBIT} \times 100}{\text{sales}} \times \frac{\text{sales}}{\text{total assets}}$$

Return on sales measures the productivity of the costs incurred in producing the company's sales revenue and asset turnover the productivity of the assets employed in the process. Both these factors which between them determine the earning power of your enterprise are key indicators of your present or planned operational efficiency.

> As indicator of present and future earning power the return on investment is perhaps the most important statement that can be made about an enterprise. Consequently it must be expected to be a leading criterion in rating your firm.

It may be instructive to trace your company's earning power back to its contributing elements in the figure that follows.

The elements of earning power

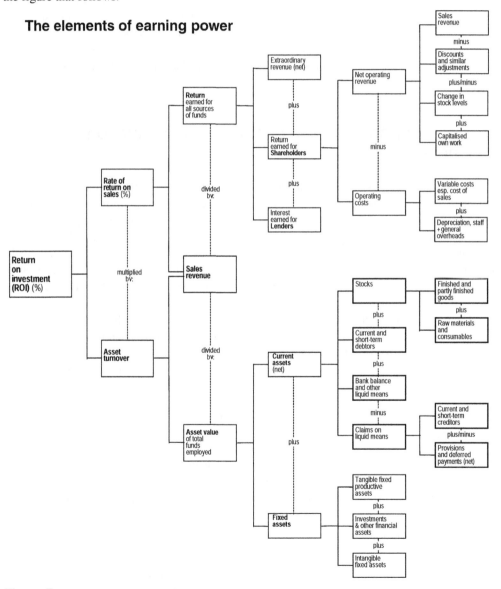

Figure 7

Focus number two: Cash flow and liquid reserves

For the rater as assessor of credit risk projections of cash flow and liquid reserves are of even greater immediate concern than the return on investment, although earning power and cash generation are, of course, closely related. It is, after all, the cash flow that enables the company to pay interest and repay the principal on due dates.

The term cash implies means of payment, but, for the purposes of financial analysis includes assets which can be converted into cash with a high degree of certainty and within a short space of time, for instance, treasury bonds or high quality trade bills.

Liquid reserves are the sum of such liquid assets minus the sum of short-term payment obligations.

Of particular interest in cash flow analysis is the 'disposable' cash flow, that is, the part of the total flow that is not absorbed by current payment obligations and can be used at management's discretion.

The analysis will take care to eliminate 'ghost flows', that is, illusionary cash flows created by book entries affecting the value of assets and liabilities, notably depreciation and similar revaluations.

The principle is illustrated in the following figure.

The sources of cash flow

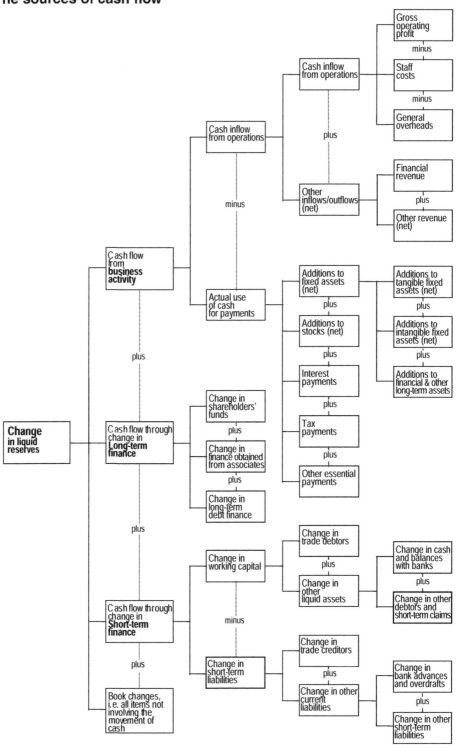

Figure 8

15 *Instruments of Financial Navigation*

For keeping your performance on the plotted course you depend on an internal information system by which to review – and, if necessary, adjust – the compass settings by which to steer your enterprise. Not all relevant information will ever be truly up to date. Projection techniques are not only needed to plot the future but merely to grasp the present. An effectively instrumented 'controlling cockpit' is indispensable in creating confidence in your ability to manage risk.

Designing plan scenarios

In order to serve its purpose as the basis for a constructive exchange with your rater your financial plan should meet the following conditions:

- Your plan will be expected to make two processes transparent: first, the process by which your business activity generates returns (in the analysis of income and expenditure) and, second, the process by which it affects the level and structure of your productive investments and their funding (in the analysis of assets and liabilities).
- A rater's interest will naturally be attracted to your projections of cash flow. These should identify, in sufficient detail, the sources and uses of cash and the ways in which the resulting flows affect size and composition of your liquid reserves.
- As an aspect of transparency the salient contents of your plan should be easy to absorb. This implies the need to be concise, but also the ability to supply exhaustive information on data sources and plan parameters which presupposes a well-organised and readily accessible background documentation.

Quantifying your assumptions

The quantification of financial plan scenarios requires the projection of the data commonly presented in the dual format of income statement and balance sheet. As a time unit for the projections the financial year is a convenient choice because it ties in neatly with the reporting cycle stipulated by commercial and tax laws. However, for financial planning and controlling over the near term, yearly projections are far too crude. For one thing, they hide the seasonal cycle which can be very pronounced in certain industries. In most cases, effective controlling will require data capture at intervals not exceeding one month. The variance of intra-month cash flow patterns may even demand controlling updates at shorter, such as weekly, intervals.

Presentations of financial plans in support of loan requests and investment offers are generally expected to cover a projection period of no less than five years and, where possible, include three to five years of history on a yearly basis. In all probability, bankers will, in addition, ask for cash flow projections for, at least, a two-year period on a monthly basis. For reasons of economy, it may, therefore, be best to base your planning and reporting routine on monthly data which will serve the purposes of both, near-term and long-term projections.

Limitations of statistical method

For practical reasons of data capturing, a company's financial information system cannot be expected ever to be truly up to date. Consequently, analysing the current situation implies the application of forecasting techniques. Obviously, the further removed from the base of actual data the greater the error margin of your forecasts.

There is an important proviso to bear in mind when applying statistical forecasting methods or interpreting their results.

Statistical methods are no more than tools for data processing. They cannot be expected, by themselves, to produce anything resembling certainty about the future.

There is one thing about statistical forecasts that can be stated with absolute certainty: they will never come true, except by coincidence.

The circumspect use of statistical method can reduce the margin of human error and help to eliminate misconceived hypotheses. Information technology greatly assists the making of forecasts, but it cannot alter the fact that its data input relates to the past. In particular, in the field of economics and finance experience has it that the mathematical sophistication of statistical method and the volume of input data are not the key to forecasting accuracy. The more effective way of improving accuracy is to increase the frequency of your forecasts and, thereby, enable a feedback loop in which your observation of patterns and trends continually adjusts your forecasts

Business forecasting is much like shooting at a moving target that waves about in an only vaguely recognisable pattern while steadily advancing towards your position. If you need to hit the target before it is getting too close, your best strategy is to keep shooting at it, constantly adjusting your aim by whatever predictable element you might discern in its movements. Thereby, your chance of hitting it rather sooner than later is maximised. In practice however, it is never a single target but a whole swarm of them you have to cope with simultaneously. Inevitably, this severely limits the time available for dealing with the individual one.

This very real constraint and the diminishing returns of analytical effort suggest a pragmatic approach to forecasting in business. Yet, for all its limitations, forward planning has proved hugely superior to the alternative of dealing reactively to events as they occur.

Key planning targets

In business, forecasting means plotting a feasible path by which to approach the goals of its mission. In most cases the process will begin with setting one or more central targets that appear attainable under calculable conditions in the near term.

The measure of success in business is profitability expressed as return on investment. The first contributor to that return is the volume of sales. Naturally, therefore, the key targets of your business plan will be sales targets, expressed in terms of volume or growth. We have seen that two main factors determine the profitability of a business: the productive efficiency of its assets and the cost efficiency of its sales, expressed in terms of return on sales and asset turnover, respectively (see page 90ff.). Figure 7 on page 94 illustrates the interaction of factors driving these two chief components.

This generic system of causation that produces profitability provides the basic blueprint also for your business plan. The elements of the system constitute the subsidiary targets of your plan, and the assumptions made about their interdependence and interaction are the parameters that tie the elements together in a dynamic model of your enterprise. Changing any of those parameters provides you with a measure of its relative influence on the overall result.

Monitoring performance vs plan

Monitoring the performance of the elements over time will suggest revisions of your plan parameters in a continual process of adaptation and fine-tuning. Your controlling dashboard will consist of selective 'information windows' through which to keep a close watch on the most potent generators of success or failure. The benefit derived from the monitoring routine is not merely that of an early warning system. Even more important is the 'experience curve' by which constant monitoring improves the efficacy of managerial reaction to its signals. With time, your plan will thus become an increasingly powerful tool of risk management. Understandably, your controlling cockpit will receive special attention by anybody rating the credit risk of your enterprise.

It goes without saying that plans compiled at lengthy intervals, for instance yearly, or as a one-time exercise in support of a financing project, have little if any practical value. What truly matters is the frequency of updates and the continuity of monitoring.

Model economy and robustness

For the reasons discussed, the essence of defining your plan parameters is not methodical sophistication but rational pragmatism. The methods described below may strike you as surprisingly simple, but you will find them quite adequate for the practical purposes of our task.

For economy and robustness a planning model should be constructed such that the chore of entering time series of individually estimated data elements (such as monthly values for a number of years) is reduced to a minimum. This is achieved by making as many data elements as possible arithmetically dependent on as small a set of input elements as the existence of actual interrelationships permits. In modelling jargon this means that a maximum of dependent variables is defined by a minimum of independent variables. Instead of an absolute value for each term of a dependent variable the determining parameter to be applied to the independent variable in the form of an additive or multiplicative constant is entered.

If your business has a track record of financial data, the historical relationships between dependent and independent variables will suggest suitable values for the constants. If you plan for a start-up, you will use your judgement and experience and, possibly, comparable industry data, to establish your first set of plan parameters. Periodic, for instance, monthly, data updates are only required for the independent variables. The constants of a model are, of course, never absolutely constant, but tend to drift with time. To adjust them for such drifts is part of the fine-tuning process.

Technically, it is possible to define the model by one single input variable on which all other elements are made dependent. That input variable will most likely be the sales volume. In practice, certain givens, such as assets that must be considered as fixed over a number of planning periods, will require independent estimates. Obviously, variables in a model that remain fixed for lengthy periods constitute limitations of productive capacity and, hence, on sales growth, as is often the case in reality. A model structure driven exclusively by the sales variable, though implying an unrealistic flexibility in all other elements, might prove useful in projecting 'ideal' capacity conditions as an aid to plotting time-critical paths for relevant action. The dynamics of certain productive processes often suggest chains of dependency in which dependant variables become the determinants of other dependent variables.

Simple model arithmetic

As a technical tool for building your planning model all you need is a spreadsheet calculator, such as the popular Microsoft Excel. Sophisticated and complex planning software is available, but you are likely to find that it is easier to work with a model of your own design in which you yourself control every step of the process.

There are a few standard items of planning arithmetic that are very easy to apply. In fact, there are basically three which, by suitable variation and combination, can be made to describe, adequately for the purpose, most dependencies between variables you might wish to project.

Simple methods of plan arithmetic

Case A:

Assuming a proportional relationship between the dependent and the determining variable.

Method: The rate of change in the independent variable is applied to the dependent variable.

Example 1:
   Expenditure on raw materials
   = X percent of sales revenue

Example 2:
   Trade creditors
   = X months of average expenditure on raw materials
   = (expenditure on raw materials for the year / 12) $\times$ X

In both examples X is the plan parameter

Case B:

Assuming a non-proportional relationship between the dependent and the determining variable.

Method: A change in the independent variable by 100% causes a change of X% in the dependent variable, where X may be smaller or greater than 100%.

Example:
   Change in advertising expenditure
   = X% of the percentage change in sales revenue

This form of dependency is frequently encountered with items of general overhead expenditure. These are commonly referred to as 'fixed' costs, but can, in reality, be observed to react in various degrees of sensitivity to a determining variable, especially sales growth.

Case C:

Assuming threshold values in the determining variable to trigger a stepwise adjustment of the dependent variable.

Method: The determining variable attaining or exceeding a certain absolute value or changing by an absolute amount or percentage Y causes the dependent variable either to equal a certain value X or to change by, optionally, an absolute value or a percentage X.

Example 1:
   Cost of administrative staff
   = X1 while sales revenue is >= Y1 and < Y2
   = X2 while sales revenue is >= Y2 and < Y3
   etc.

Example 2:
   Investment in new plant
   = X1 new investment when sales revenue exceeds Y1
   = X2 new investment when sales revenue exceeds Y2
   etc.

This method of obtaining a stepwise adjustment of the dependent variable to a trigger value reached by the determining variable will in most practical planning situations prove unnecessary. Especially, where the business unit under consideration is not too large and the determining variable an originally independent one, it will be easier and more efficient to enter the new value of the dependent variable directly in the planning schedule.

Panel 29

We have earlier discussed the principle of translating a strategy into the terms of a financial plan. You will have quantified the chief goals of your strategy, for instance, sales revenue from certain markets, not merely as distant targets, but as series of periodic, preferably monthly, values plotting the path towards them. Correspondingly, you will have drawn up a plan of action in relevant key result areas to realise these targets and quantified that action in terms of expenditure and investment along the time axis of your plan. These quantities you will, of course, enter directly in your planning spreadsheet.

Once the input variables and constants are in place, the chore of updating and adjusting the system reduces literally to a matter of minutes. A particularly useful feature of the spreadsheet powered planning model is that it is interactive. It makes it easy to set up and test alternative scenarios, for instance, when exploring best case or worst case potentials.

16 A Rational Look at Your Financial Future

Once your bankers have accepted your assessment of your business potential, their interest will shift to the conditions, especially the financial conditions, under which the proposed mechanics of realising it may be exploited to the full. Their questions will centre on your ability to influence the critical conditions of success which your strategic plan has identified. The worked example of plan construction included in this chapter helps you to anticipate those questions and prepare conclusive answers.

Your financial plan drawn up in the manner outlined above as a holistic model of your business and its projected development will contain the answers. They are reflected in its elements and, especially, in the parameters describing their interaction. Although presented in the conventional format of income statement and balance sheet, its design will have been guided by the recognised potentials of controlling the conditions of your company's success. To aid identification of these potentials we have considered the scope for controlling action by key result areas (pages 74ff.).

Here follows a sample of typical issues raised in discussions of financial plans listed by major domain of strategic action:

1. **Income generation (primary strategies)**
    1.1 **Marketing and distribution**
        The sales targets
        The assumptions underlying the sales targets
        Pricing
        Direct costs
        Costs of advertising and promotion
        Costs of distribution
    1.2 **Products and product development**
        Intended investment in research facilities
        Cost of specialist staff
        Cost of rights and licences
    1.3 **Operational organisation and processes**
        Intended modernisation of plant
        Intended investment to increase output capacity
        Planned backward and forward linkages
        Intended mergers with or acquisitions of other companies
        Change in location

2. Resources (secondary strategies)
  2.1 Production
     Direct costs of production
     Costs of warehousing and distribution
     Changes in stocks of processed and finished goods
  2.2 Supplies
     Costs of obtaining input materials and services
     Prices of raw materials
     Change in stocks of materials
  2.3 Personnel
     Cost of executive staff
     Cost of operating staff by category and function
     Trend in salary levels
  2.4 Finance
     Sources of finance
     Kinds and terms of finance employed
     Funding of intended strategic investments
     Interest rates paid and received.

This chapter addresses the problem of designing your financial plan in such a manner as to serve two important purposes at once. The first is to collect, process and analyse your financial data in sufficient depth to meet all conceivable requirements for rating the financial strength and risk of your enterprise. The other is to provide you with an effective medium for communicating the salient features of your financial plan to bankers and other interested parties.

One important practical condition for ensuring that your plan can serve your bankers as source of input data for their rating procedure is that its contents are conveniently organised. An effective way of achieving this is to structure your presentation in tiers representing successive levels of disaggregation of information from a two-page summary of income statement and balance sheet downwards.

The chapter contains a set of Plansheets with explanatory comments to guide you in the dual task of compiling a conclusive analysis and presenting a 'readable' documentation. They are intended as illustrative examples, but will also serve as templates for you to pare down to suit your particular requirements.

Main heads of analysis

The main heads of financial analysis were summarised on pages 90 to 92. The following discussion is organised in the same manner, that is, under these headings:

I.   Income and expenditure
II.   Investment and funding
III. Financial structure
IV. Cash flow and liquid reserves
V.   Rating indicators

PRAGMATICS OF PRESENTATION

The basic format of a financial plan is the conventional combination of income statement and balance sheet. However, the content is arranged to serve the purposes of analysis, that is, not any particular set of rules governing accepted practice of accounting and financial reporting in any particular country.

The terminology used in this book is eclectic, especially that which is used in the following example of a financial plan and its analysis. From among the various national sets of financial jargon with preferences shaped by local accounting practice as well as commercial and tax legislation, those expressions have been selected that cause the least problems of interpretation for the person not professionally familiarised with the subject. Although the principles of accounting and analysis are the same the world over, there does not as yet exist a definitive nomenclature. In your own approach to financial planning you should, therefore, feel free to use the terms of your preference.

In plan presentations, digital accuracy beyond the limit of significance has no merit. It is not merely spurious but reduces legibility. Insignificant digits should be rounded off. Wherever feasible they should be eliminated by presenting the data in thousands or millions of the currency unit.

The worked example included in the following tables demonstrates the arithmetic of the analysis as might be replicated on a spreadsheet. Reference codes in the right-hand margin identify the individual data items in cross-references. The example covers one analysis period (from the balance sheet per the end of period 0 through the income statement for the period 1 to the balance sheet per the end of that period). That period might be taken as one month, one quarter or one year or any other space of time. The analysis is essentially the same in every case, with the proviso that comparisons of intra-yearly periods might be difficult to interpret because of seasonal variations, which can be severe, unless one is prepared to go to the trouble of seasonally adjusting the data.

A TECHNICAL NOTE

In case you are tempted to try out the analysis demonstrated below on your PC using a standard spreadsheet calculator and your own data, here is a suggestion of how to avoid two potentially awkward calculation problems:

Making your plan balance sheets balance

If you enter historical balance sheet data in your spreadsheet, the sum of assets will, by definition, always equal the sum of liabilities unless there has been a transcription error. Not so, except by highly unlikely coincidence, if you enter individually projected plan data, whether in absolute values or via formulae defining dependencies on determining variables. Such differences between total assets and total liabilities in your plan imply a surplus or deficit of cash which ought to be reflected as hypothetical credit or debit balances in your bank account, thereby balancing the balance sheet.

This is achieved by making bank balances on current account the residual item of your plan calculations as follows: define both positive balances (assets) and negative balances (liabilities) as the difference between all other assets and liabilities. Enter surpluses of cash as positive balance with your bank on the asset side and shortfalls as negative balance on the liability side of your plan balance sheet. By way of the relational 'If' operator of your spreadsheet software the process can be automated.

Balances on current account should preferably be in your credit, but not larger than needed for day-to-day financial transactions, in order to avoid a waste of possibly expensive funds in low-return or no-return uses. Large credit or debit balances resulting from your planning exercise will, therefore, suggest an adjustment of other asset or liability items in your plan.

> Making current bank balances the residual of your planning model is a particularly useful feature in the early stages of testing your plan. At a stage when no assumptions have yet been made regarding additional funds required to finance the plan, a negative bank balance showing up in the test indicates the total amount of new finance needed to satisfy all the other assumptions that define your model.

Escaping the 'circular reference' loop

Financial planning requires you to link the data sets of successive periods in one continuous analysis which you may wish to extend from some point in history to the time horizon of your plan. By general accounting practice, the linkage is effected by carrying forward the taxed net profit or loss for one period to the opening balance sheet of the next period, where it increases or decreases, respectively, the amount of shareholders' funds, specifically the balance on the profit and loss account included among the capital accounts on the liabilities side of the balance sheet.

Unfortunately, the expedient of making the bank balance on current account the residual item of the plan causes a problem for the spreadsheet software: the interest that the current account balance costs or earns is calculated by multiplying the balance with the appropriate interest factor. The interest entered in the income statement changes the profit, and the change brought forward to the balance sheet upsets the equality of assets and liability which the system compensates by changing the current account balance. This change, in turn, requires a re-calculation of the interest, thereby completing a 'circular reference' loop. Your standard spreadsheet is unlikely to be equipped with the highly complex matrix calculus facility required for solving circular reference problems and will refuse the operation.

The alternative solution is by iteration. This sounds tedious, but, fortunately for our practical purposes, is very easy to accomplish: perform the interest calculation in a side calculation on your spreadsheet and enter the result by hand in the appropriate place on the income statement. Theoretically, this process is to be repeated several times until the repetition yields no significant improvement of the fit between the planned rate of interest and the one implied by the amount of interest entered. However, because of your obvious endeavour to keep current account balances at a minimum, the relevant interest charges will tend to be relatively small to begin with and, in most cases, you are likely to find that already your first entry results in an adequately close approximation.

Performing the projections

Here follows the example of a comprehensive financial analysis and its presentation. All projections of variables considered dependent on a determining variable are assumed to be made in terms of the methods described on page 101 as Cases A, B and C.

OVERVIEW OF RESULTS AND YOUR STATE OF FINANCE

The part of your financial plan that will draw the first critical attention of your raters is the summary. It is the top tier of your plan structure. To serve its purpose, it should not exceed two pages, one each for income statement and balance sheet.

Here follows a sample. As you see from the cross-references, every item in the summary is brought forward from a separately tabulated modular plan on a lower level of aggregation.

Income statement

Reference
code

I. Income and expenditure

cross-referenced to the detailed analysis on Plansheets 3 to 10

	Period t-1	Period t	
Revenue source 1		12 469	*110.1*
Revenue source 2		8 313	*110.2*
Revenue source 3		5 195	*110.3*
Total revenue (Plansheet 3)	**19 743**	**25 977**	**110.**
+/- Other revenue and adjustments (net) (Plansheet 3)		-95	*120.*
Operating income (Plansheet 3)		**25 882**	**100.**
- Cost of sales (Plansheet 3)		14 625	*210.*
Gross operating profit (Plansheet 3)	**6 820**	**11 257**	**200.**
Provisions for depreciation (Plansheet 4)		969	*310.*
Staff costs (Plansheet 6)		3 926	*320.*
General overheads (Plansheet 7)		3 276	*330.*
- Total fixed operating costs		8 171	*300.*
- Short-term provisions for liabilities (net) (Plansheet 8)		78	*410.*
+ Other operating revenue (net) (Plansheet 8)		-84	*510.*
Net operating profit (Plansheet 8)		**2 924**	**500.**
- Financial costs and revenue (net) (Plansheet 9)		48	*600.*
+ Extraordinary income and expenditure (net) Plansheet 10)		5	*700.*
Net profit before tax (Plansheet 10)		**2 881**	**920.**
- Taxation (Plansheet 10)		1 354	*800.*
Net profit after tax (Plansheet 10)		**1 527**	**900.**

Plansheet 1

Balance sheet

Reference
code

II. Investment and funding

cross-referenced to the detailed analysis on Plansheets 12 to 17

	Period t-1	Period t	
Investment (assets)			
Tangible fixed assets (Plansheet 12)	3 601	3 685	*1110.1*
Intangible fixed assets (Plansheet 12)	206	145	*1110.2*
Investments in associated companies (Plansheet 13)	745	615	*1120.*
Long-term financial investments (Plansheet 13)	185	203	*1130.*
Other long-term assets (Plansheet 13)	6	8	*1140.*
Fixed assets (Plansheet 13)	**4 743**	**4 656**	*1100.*
Stocks (Plansheet 14)	358	708	*1210.*
Trade debtors (Plansheet 14)	523	1 253	*1221.*
Other current assets (Plansheet 14)	158	220	*1222.*
Cash and balances with banks (Plansheet 14)	32	482	*1223.*
Working capital (Plansheet 14)	713	1 955	*1220.*
Current assets (Plansheet 14)	**1 071**	**2 663**	*1200.*
Total investment	**5 814**	**7 319**	*1000.*
Funding (liabilities)			
Shareholders' capital	850	850	*2110.*
Profit and loss account	-337	190	*2120.*
Shareholders' loans and capital type investments	1 350	1 400	*2130.*
Shareholders' funds (Plansheet 15)	**1 863**	**2 440**	*2100.*
Provisions (Plansheet 15)	**668**	**1 435**	*2210.*
Associated companies (Plansheet 16)	220	225	*2220.*
Long-term debt (Plansheet 16)	2 172	1 973	*2230.*
Trade creditors (Plansheet 17)	479	569	*2241.*
Other current liabilities (Plansheet 17)	163	295	*2242.*
Bank advances and overdrafts (Plansheet 17)	249	382	*2243.*
Current liabilities (Plansheet 17)	891	1 246	*2240.*
Total debt	**3 283**	**3 444**	*2200.*
Total funding	**5 814**	**7 319**	*2000.*

Plansheet 2

FROM REVENUE TO GROSS PROFIT

Gross operating profit is defined as total turnover after subtraction of all adjustments and costs that directly relate to the processes generating it.

In many companies revenue is broken down into strategic categories by criteria such as product group, class of business, geographical origin, destination etc. These may imply significant differences in the proportion and composition of the relevant cost of sales. In such cases, the analysis of operational efficiency requires separately prepared income statements up to the level of gross operating profit for each category.

Operating income

Sales revenue is defined as per prices charged, net of direct taxes such as sales tax or value added tax (VAT). In most cases revenue is the primary strategic target and, thus, the chief independent variable of the plan. Total revenue (total turnover) is usually the most comprehensive indicator of business activity.

Projection method:	As alternative to absolute inputs.
Determinant:	Total or relevant sectoral sales revenue for the previous period.
Dependency:	Change through a period.
Parameter:	Percentage of determinant.

Adjustments to sales revenue are made for discounts and rebates and any other charges that have the effect of modifying sales prices.

Projection method:	
Determinant:	Total or relevant sectoral sales revenue.
Dependency:	Proportional change.
Parameter:	Percentage of determinant.

Variable operating costs

Cost of sales the most important category in this module, includes costs such as raw materials, purchased components and external services used in producing the goods and services sold, but also direct costs of distribution such as packaging, freight and insurance.

Projection method:	
Determinant:	Total or relevant sectoral sales revenue.
Dependency:	Proportional change.
Parameter:	Percentage of determinant.

I. Income and expenditure

(1 of 8)

Reference
code

1. Operating income

Revenue
by source (product, market, business unit etc.):

Source 1	12 469	*110.1*
Source 2	8 313	*110.2*
Source 3	5 195	*110.3*
etc.		

	25 977	**110.**

- Discounts allowed etc.	-208	*121.*
+/- Change in inventories	-6	*122.*
+ Capitalised own work	23	*123.*
+ Sundry operating revenue	96	*124.*

Other revenue and adjustments (net)	-95	*120.*

Operating Income	**25 882**	***100.***

2. Variable operating costs

Cost of sales
*if differences warrant, by source
(product, market, business unit etc.):*
specifically:

Raw materials and components	8 754	*211.*
External services	156	*212.*
Freight	104	*213.*
Commissions	5 611	*214.*
etc.		

	14 625	*210.*

Gross operating profit	**11 257**	***200.***

Plansheet 3

OPERATING COSTS AND OPERATING PROFIT

Net operating profit is defined as gross operating profit after subtraction of all operating costs which are not expected to vary directly, that is, in proportional correlation with sales revenue.

Fixed operating costs

These costs are fixed in the sense that they typically do not change in response to changes in sales revenue. They reflect an important principle of business economics: the economies of scale. In reality, however, these costs are inflexible mainly on the downside, while tending to drift upward, although generally not proportionally, with increasing turnover.

AMORTISATION OF FIXED ASSETS

Provision for depreciation charged against assets with a relatively long but limited useful life is usually regulated by national legislation, notably tax legislation. Such assets may be tangible (such as plant, machinery and vehicles) or intangible (such as patents and rights). For our present purposes, it is mainly the economic life of an asset that matters, not the technical or functional one.

> *Projection method:*
> *Determinant:* The relevant fixed assets.
> *Dependency:* Fraction of the original (e.g. at purchase) value, or the current value of the determinant.
> *Parameter:* Alternatively, percentage of the determinant or the value of the determinant divided by the estimated number of periods of its estimated life. (Where the depreciation schedule is known, absolute inputs may be preferred.)

EMPLOYMENT AND STAFF COSTS

Numbers of employees tend to increase with the volume of business, but usually not proportionally with sales revenue. Employment will adjust more flexibly in the areas of production and distribution than in administration.

> *Projection method:*
> *Determinant:* Mainly relevant sectoral sales revenue.
> *Dependency:* Sub-proportional change.
> *Parameter:* Rate of growth for the period expressed as a fraction (percentage) of the percentage growth of the determinant.

Staff costs in a particular category are determined by numbers of staff and the relevant salary level.

    Projection method:
        Determinant A: Number of employees in a predefined category.
        Determinant B: Average salary in the relevant category for the period. (The schedule of applicable salaries is usually an independent input.)
        Dependency: Direct definition by determinants A and B.
        Parameter: B applied as multiplier to the value of A.

OVERHEADS

General operating costs increase in varying degrees of sensitivity to increases in business activity, but tend to resist reduction in periods of declining turnover.

    Projection method:
        Case 1:   Standard sub-proportional response of costs to increases in business volume.
        Determinant: Mainly relevant sectoral sales revenue.
        Dependency: Sub-proportional change.
        Parameter: Rate of growth for the period expressed as a fraction (percentage) of the percentage growth of the determinant.

        Case 2:   For certain costs which remain genuinely fixed for longer periods such as property leases, rent and building maintenance.
        Determinant: Current values.
        Dependency: Value for previous period.
        Parameter: Equality (repetition).

        Case 3:   For certain overheads in production, distribution and administration.
        Determinant: The relevant number of employees.
        Dependency: Proportional change.
        Parameter: Percentage of determinant.

Operating profit

Net operating profit is arrived at by subtracting from gross operating profit the fixed operating costs, that is, depreciation, staff costs and general overheads, and adding other business related revenue not yet accounted for.

Other business-related revenue/costs consists of various incidental items such as short-term provisions for amounts payable and other business related costs or revenues. These are items frequently found in historical income statements. In most cases they are insignificant and can be neglected in plans.

Projection method:
Determinant: Total sales revenue.
Dependency: Proportional change.
Parameter: Percentage of determinant.

I. Income and expenditure

(2 of 8)   Reference
                                                                        code

3. Fixed operating costs

3.1 Provisions for depreciation of fixed assets
Itemisation compatible with that of the relevant assets (Plansheet 12)

Tangible assets

    Land and buildings
      specifically (e.g.):

Location 1	38	*310.111*
Location 2	5	*310.112*
Location 3	27	*310.113*
etc.		
	70	***310.11***

    Machinery, plant and equipment
      specifically (e.g.):

Production unit 1	182	*310.121*
Production unit 2	105	*310.122*
Production unit 3	99	*310.123*
etc.		
	386	***310.12***

    Furniture and fittings
      specifically (e.g.):

Production	203	*310.131*
Warehousing	158	*310.132*
Offices	27	*310.133*
etc.		
	388	***310.13***

    Vehicles
      specifically (e.g.):

Staff cars	14	*310.141*
Transport vehicles	7	*310.142*
etc.		
	21	***310.14***

Depreciation of tangible fixed assets	**865**	***310.1***

Intangible assets
   specifically (e.g.):

Goodwill	0	*310.21*
Rights, licenses etc.	42	*310.22*
Computer software	62	*310.23*
etc.		
	104	***310.2***

Total provision for depreciation	**969**	***310.***

Plansheet 4

I. Income and expenditure

(3 of 8)   Reference
                                            code

3. Fixed operating costs (continued)

3.2 Employment and staff costs

3.2.1 Numbers of employees

Production
specifically:

Management	1	*321.11*
Technical and related administration	5	*321.12*
Operators category 1	6	*321.131*
Operators category 2	3	*321.132*
Operators category 3	5	*321.133*
Other	1	*321.14*
	21	*321.1*

Marketing and sales
specifically:

Management	2	*321.21*
Assistants	4	*321.22*
Sales staff	11	*321.23*
	17	*321.2*

Administration
specifically:

Management	2	*321.31*
Management assistants	4	*321.32*
Professional staff	4	*321.33*
Secretariat and office	2	*321.34*
	12	*321.3*

Total number employed	50	*321.*

Plansheet 5

I. Income and expenditure

(4 of 8)

3. Fixed operating costs (continued)

3.2 Employment and staff costs (continued)

3.2.2 Staff costs

Production
specifically:

Management	122	*320.11*
Technical and related administration	330	*320.12*
Operators category 1	456	*320.13*
Operators category 2	192	*320.14*
Operators category 3	300	*320.15*
Other	40	*320.16*
	1 440	***320.1***

Marketing and sales
specifically:

Management	244	*320.21*
Assistants	288	*320.22*
Sales staff	1 056	*320.23*
	1 588	***320.2***

Administration
specifically:

Management	244	*320.31*
Management assistants	240	*320.32*
Professional staff	292	*320.33*
Secretariat and office	122	*320.34*
	898	***320.3***

Total staff costs	**3 926**	***320.***

Plansheet 6

I. Income and expenditure

(5 of 8)

Reference code

3. Fixed operating costs (continued)

3.3 General overheads

Production
specifically:

Cost of premises	472	*331.1*
Energy and water	413	*331.2*
Consumables	177	*331.3*
Maintenance and repairs	133	*331.4*
Services	221	*331.5*
Other	59	*331.9*
	1 474	***331.***

Marketing and sales
specifically:

Cost of premises	157	*332.1*
Office overheads	138	*332.2*
Advertising media	334	*332.3*
Public relations	128	*332.4*
Catalogues, brochures etc.	88	*332.5*
Travel expenses	98	*332.6*
Other	39	*332.9*
	983	***332.***

Administration
specifically:

Cost of premises	188	*333.1*
Office overheads	287	*333.2*
Appliance leasing	156	*333.3*
Staff training	49	*333.4*
Memberships and insurance	41	*333.5*
Legal and other consulting services	33	*333.6*
Travel expenses	49	*333.7*
Other	16	*333.9*
	819	***333.***

Total overheads	**3 276**	***330.***

Plansheet 7

I. Income and expenditure

(6 of 8)

Reference code

4. Operating profit

Gross operating profit (c/f from Plansheet 3)	**11 257**	*200.*
Provision for depreciation (c/f from Plansheet 4)	969	*310.*
Staff costs (c/f from Plansheet 6)	3 926	*320.*
General overheads (c/f from Plansheet 7)	3 276	*330.*
Total fixed operating costs	8 171	*300.*
- Short-term provisions for liabilities (net)*	78	*410.*
Net operating profit I	**3 008**	*400.*
+ Other business related revenue*	43	*511.*
- Revaluation of assets other than depreciation*	-102	*512.*
- Other business related costs*	-25	*513.*
+/- Other business related revenue/costs (net)	-84	*510.*
Net operating profit II	**2 924**	*500.*

* if amounts warrant, specify

Plansheet 8

FINANCIAL CHARGES AND SHAREHOLDERS' PROFIT

Net profit as the return earned for shareholders (which may be negative) is defined as net operating profit after financial charges and any extraordinary amounts payable or receivable.

Financial costs and revenue are related to the relevant financial assets and liabilities in the balance sheet by independently projected interest rates.

Projection method:

Case 1:   Interest charged on the original amount of the principal.

Determinant A: Average value of the financial asset or liability for the period.

Determinant B: Independent estimate of the relevant interest rate.

Dependency: Proportional change.

Parameter: Average A multiplied by interest factor B.

Case 2:   Interest charged on currently changing debt balances and on debt reduced by periodic repayments.

Determinant A: Average value of the financial asset or liability for the period.

Determinant B: Independent estimate of the relevant interest rate.

Dependency: Proportional change.

Parameter: Average A multiplied by interest factor B.

With certain forms of long-term debt such as mortgage finance periodic repayments and interest are combined in a fixed amount. In such cases future interest payments can be obtained from a payment schedule separating redemption from interest.

Case 3:   Interest included in mortgage type fixed service charges on long-term debt.

Determinant: None (independently determined payment schedule).

Dependency: None.

Parameter: None (absolute value entries).

Extraordinary income and expenditure is, by its nature, not predictable. In this category belong gains and losses from currency transactions, one-time subsidies, uninsured losses by accident, book gains on sales of assets etc. In instances, extraordinary items can be substantial and distort the analysis. For the purposes of assessing profitability and risk, any revenue and expenditure not related to the company's ordinary business should be collected under this head. Such items as are already known to occur in a future period will be entered as absolute values.

> *Projection method:*
> > *Determinant:*   None (if included at all, independently
> > determined data).
> > *Dependency:*   None.
> > *Parameter:*   None (absolute value entry).

Taxation in this context is essentially a charge against income. Direct tax such as sales tax or value added tax (VAT) is charged against gross revenue. (As is the case in our example, sales revenue in financial plans is usually defined as net of direct taxes.) Corporate income tax in its various forms is typically defined as a percentage on net profit, possibly with certain modifications. There can be other forms of taxation such as on certain types of assets or capital. In either case projections are made accordingly.

> *Projection method:*
> > *Determinant:*   Usually net profit, in certain cases asset or
> > liability items.
> > *Dependency:*   Proportional change.
> > *Parameter:*   Percentage of determinant.

I. Income and expenditure

Reference
code

5. Financial costs and revenue

Financial costs
Interest, discounts and similar charges

by source, e.g.:

Shareholders' loans (2131., Plansheet 15)	20	*611.*
Long-term loans (2231., Plansheet 16)	88	*613.*
Loans from associated companies (2221., Plansheet 16)	10	*612.*
Trade creditors (2241., Plansheet 17)	51	*614.*
Bank credit on current account (2243.1, Plansheet 17)	0	*615.*
Other bank credit (2243.2, Plansheet 17)	31	*616.*

Total financial costs   **200**   *610.*

Financial revenue
Interest, discounts, dividends etc.

by source, e.g.:

Shares in associated companies (1121., Plansheet 13)	15	*621.*
Loans to associated companies (1122., Plansheet 13)	5	*622.*
Securities (1131., Plansheet 13)	3	*623.*
Long-term loans (1132., Plansheet 13)	5	*624.*
Other long-term financial investments (1133., Plansheet 13)	1	*625.*
Trade debtors (1221., Plansheet 14)	107	*626.*
Liquid investments (1222.1, Plansheet 14)	5	*627.*
Current balances with banks (1223.1, Plansheet 14)	1	*628.*
Deposits etc. with banks (1223.2, Plansheet 14)	10	*629.*

Total financial revenue   **152**   *620.*

Financial costs and revenue (net)   **-48**   *600.*

Plansheet 9

I. Income and expenditure

(8 of 8)

6. Shareholders' profit

		Reference code
Net operating profit II (c/f from Plansheet 8)	2 924	*500.*
- Financial costs (c/f from Plansheet 9)	200	*610.*
+ Financial revenue (net) (c/f from Plansheet 9)	152	*620.*
+ Extraordinary income and expenditure (net) *	5	*700.*
Net profit/loss before tax	2 881	*910.*
Corporate income tax	1 210	*810.*
Other taxation of income or assets	144	*820.*
- Total taxes	1 354	*800.*
Net profit/loss after tax	1 527	*900.*

---

* if amounts warrant, specify

Plansheet 10

INVESTMENT IN PRODUCTIVE ASSETS

Fixed assets are assets with a life extending over several years and assumed, by economic rationale, to depreciate gradually to a zero value. The process is emulated in the company's accounts by periodic charges against the book value of the relevant assets. A point to bear in mind is that the financial depreciation applied in accounting is typically defined by tax laws rather than individual assessments of economic life. Financial depreciation in excess of decreases in market value creates hidden reserves for the benefit of shareholders, while insufficiently depreciated, hence overvalued, assets overstate the net worth of shareholders' interest. Raters will look out for conspicuous deviations of the book value of fixed assets from their market value.

New investments for historical periods included in the plan can be readily inferred from the book values of the relevant assets at the end of two successive periods and the depreciation charged for that period. For obvious reasons, plan values for major investments such as in land, buildings and plant are determined independently. Depending on individual circumstances, certain other assets can be made dependent on variables. For example: certain types of machinery, equipment and transport vehicles may be related to demand on output reflected in relevant items of sales revenue. Vehicles in a certain category may be related to the number of sales staff. Equipment for workstations such as PCs and furniture may be related to staff numbers in administration.

Projection method:
Case 1:	Independently determined data.
Determinant:	None.
Dependency:	None.
Parameter:	None (absolute value entry).

Case 2:	Stepwise adjustment to a determining variable.
Determinant:	Revenue from relevant source.
Dependency:	Stepwise increase upon determinant reaching a trigger value.
Parameter:	Percentage of previous value.

Case 3:	Continual adjustment to a determining variable.
Determinant:	Sectoral sales revenue or other suitable variable such as numbers of employees in certain functions.
Dependency:	Proportional change.
Parameter:	Percentage of determinant.

End-of-period asset values are implicitly determined by new investments and depreciation.

> *Projection method:*
> | | |
> |---|---|
> | *Determinant A:* | Relevant asset value at the end of the previous period. |
> | *Determinant B:* | New investment during the period. |
> | *Determinant C:* | Depreciation for the period. |
> | *Dependency:* | Implied by interaction of A, B and C. |
> | *Parameter:* | Sum: A + B - C. |

II. Investment and funding

Reference
                                                                 code

1. Investment in fixed assets

1.1 New investments
corresponding with tables of year-end values (Plansheet 12) und depreciation (Plansheet 4)

Tangible assets

Land and buildings		
specifically (e.g.):		
Location 1	0	*1111.111*
Location 2	0	*1111.112*
Location 3	300	*1111.113*
etc.		
	300	*1111.11*
Machinery, plant and equipment		
specifically (e.g.):		
Production unit 1	54	*1111.121*
Production unit 2	158	*1111.122*
Production unit 3	27	*1111.123*
etc.		
	239	*1111.12*
Furniture and fittings		
specifically (e.g.):		
Production	206	*1111.131*
Warehousing	142	*1111.132*
Offices	34	*1111.133*
etc.		
	382	*1111.13*
Vehicles		
specifically (e.g.):		
Staff cars	8	*1111.131*
Transport vehicles	20	*1111.132*
etc.		
	28	*1111.14*
New investment in tangible fixed assets	949	*1111.1*
Intangible assets		
specifically (e.g.):		
Goodwill	0	*1111.21*
Rights, licenses etc.	18	*1111.22*
Computer software	25	*1111.23*
etc.		
	43	*1111.2*
Total new investment in fixed assets	992	*1111.*

Plansheet 11

II. Investment and funding

(2 of 7)

Reference code

1. Investment in fixed assets (continued)

1.2 End-of-period asset values
for depreciation see Plansheet 4

	Period t-1	Period t	
Tangible assets			
Land and buildings			
specifically (e.g.):			
Location 1	756	718	*1110.111*
Location 2	102	97	*1110.112*
Location 3	234	507	*1110.113*
etc.			
	1 092	**1 322**	*1110.11*
Machinery, plant and equipment			
specifically (e.g.):			
Production unit 1	855	727	*1110.121*
Production unit 2	354	410	*1110.122*
Production unit 3	483	408	*1110.123*
etc.			
	1 692	**1 545**	*1110.12*
Furniture and fittings			
specifically (e.g.):			
Production	404	407	*1110.131*
Warehousing	333	317	*1110.132*
Offices	47	54	*1110.133*
etc.			
	784	**778**	*1110.13*
Vehicles			
specifically (e.g.):			
Staff cars	33	27	*1110.131*
Transport vehicles	0	13	*1110.132*
etc.			
	33	**40**	*1110.14*
Investment in tangible fixed assets	**3 601**	**3 685**	*1110.1*
Intangible assets			
specifically (e.g.):			
Goodwill	0	0	*1110.21*
Rights, licenses etc.	108	84	*1110.22*
Computer software	98	61	*1110.23*
etc.			
	206	**145**	*1110.2*
Total investment in fixed assets	**3 807**	**3 830**	*1110.*

Plansheet 12

YOUR ASSET PORTFOLIO

The assets listed in the balance sheet are traditionally organised in decreasing order of life terms.

Fixed assets

Depreciating fixed assets have already been dealt with in the preceding section and are carried forward under this head.

Investments in associated companies are of a strategic nature and enter the financial plan as inputs in absolute terms.

> *Projection method:*
>   *Determinant:*   Independently determined data.
>   *Dependency:*   None.
>   *Parameter:*   None (absolute value entry).

Long-term financial investments such as securities and loans other than those representing assistance to associates rarely reflect a firm's ordinary business activity and are not commonly part of a financial plan. It they are, they are best entered as absolute values.

> *Projection method:*
>   *Determinant:*   Independently determined data.
>   *Dependency:*   None.
>   *Parameter:*   None (absolute value entry).

Other long-term assets are a catchall item to include any long-life asset that does not fit one of the above categories and will, if at all, be projected in absolute value terms.

> *Projection method:*
>   *Determinant:*   Independently determined data.
>   *Dependency:*   None.
>   *Parameter:*   None (absolute value entry).

Current assets

Stocks serve two basic functions, ensuring the availability of goods offered in the market as well as materials and components needed for producing them. In the first instance the chief determinant is sales revenue and in the second the use of raw materials and components reflected in the cost of sales. In financial plans stock requirements are conveniently expressed as the number of periods, usually months, in which they will be turned over once in the course of ordinary business activity. Stocks tie up space and finance, and competent management will aim to minimise them by organising production and supplies wherever possible on the just-in-time principle. The kind of the firm's business may entail cyclical variations in stock levels, for example, where seasonal factors determine the timing of raw material purchases such as fresh fruit. These predictable variations can be taken into account by corresponding variations in the planning parameter.

Projection method:

Case 1:	Stocks of finished goods and work in progress.
Determinant:	Total or relevant sectoral sales revenue.
Dependency:	Multiple of the average value of the determinant over a suitable space of time (e.g. one year).
Parameter:	Number of periods (e.g. months).

Case 2:	Stocks of raw materials and consumables.
Determinant:	Total or relevant variable costs (costs of sales).
Dependency:	Multiple of the average value of the determinant over a suitable space of time (e.g. one year).
Parameter:	Number of periods (e.g. months).

Trade debtors reflect payment terms granted to customers and are usually measured in terms of periods, usually months.

Projection method:

Determinant:	Total or relevant sectoral sales revenue.
Dependency:	Multiple of the average value of the determinant over a suitable space of time (e.g. one moving quarter).
Parameter:	Number of plan periods (e.g. months).

Other current assets (other than cash and current account balances with banks), such as liquid investments and advance payments made, are usually minor items in a balance sheet. These are expediently assumed to be reduced to zero over the first or the first few plan periods or projected in terms of total business activity.

Projection method:

Determinant:	Total sales revenue.
Dependency:	Proportional change.
Parameter:	Percentage of determinant.

Cash and balances with banks will ordinarily be a marginal item on the balance sheet. In financial plans it also serves the pragmatic function of evening out differences between projections of total assets and total liabilities (see the technical note on page 105). In plan projections, consistently large balances with banks imply an unrealistic waste of liquidity and suggest a reduction of projected debt levels.

II. Investment and funding

(3 of 7)

2. Investments (assets)

2.1 Fixed assets

	Period t-1	Period t	Reference code
Tangible fixed assets (c/f from Plansheet 12)	3 601	3 685	1110.1
Intangible fixed assets (c/f from Plansheet 12)	206	145	1110.2
Depreciating fixed assets	**3 807**	**3 830**	*1110.*
Shares in associated companies	500	500	1121.
Loans to associated companies	200	100	1122.
Other claims on associated companies	45	15	1123.
Investments in associated companies	**745**	**615**	*1120.*
Securities	75	95	1131.
Long-term loans	100	100	1132.
Other long-term financial investments	10	8	1133.
Long-term financial investments	**185**	**203**	*1130.*
Other long-term assets	6	8	*1140.*
Total fixed assets	**4 743**	**4 656**	*1100.*

Plansheet 13

II. Investment and funding

(4 of 7)

2. Investments (assets)

2.2 Current assets

	Period t-1	Period t	Reference code
Work in progress and finished goods *if warranted, broken down into* *product type, business unit etc.*	65	244	1211.
Raw materials and consumable stores	293	464	1212.
Stocks	**358**	**708**	**1210.**
Trade debtors	523	1 253	1221.
Liquid investments	85	134	1222.1
Other short-term claims	17	10	1222.2
Deferred accruals/advances paid	56	76	1222.3
Other current assets	158	220	1222.
Balance on current account	0	226	1223.1
Deposits and other accounts	30	251	1223.2
Cash on hand	2	5	1223.3
Cash and balances with banks	32	482	1223.
Working capital	**713**	**1 955**	**1220.**
Total current assets	**1 071**	**2 663**	**1200.**

Plansheet 14

FINANCING YOUR ASSET PORTFOLIO

As the assets are arranged in the balance sheet in decreasing order of their economic life, the funding facilities that finance them are listed in decreasing order of their terms of availability.

Shareholders' funds

Shareholders' capital constitutes the funds that are, by definition, invested on a permanent basis. That fact makes them the focus of attention in risk analysis. The classic form of shareholders' equity is paid up shares and reserves accumulated by retaining profits. Increasing the company's capital by issuing new shares – or, under special circumstances, reducing it by repayments to shareholders – is a strategic decision of major consequence. Changes in capital are, therefore, always independent inputs to the financial plan.

> *Projection method:*
>   *Determinant:*   Independently determined data.
>   *Dependency:*   None.
>   *Parameter:*   None (absolute value entry).

The profit and loss account provides the link between income statement and balance sheet. It collects periodically the net profits or losses of current business activity and is, if not formally so, a part of the company's capital. It is from this account, that dividends are paid out to shareholders. Dividend payments are strategic decisions and enter the financial plan as externally determined absolute values.

> *Projection method:*
>   *Case 1:*   Change by current profit or loss.
>   *Determinant:*   Net profit after tax for the period.
>   *Dependency:*   Equal to determinant.
>   *Parameter:*   Equality.
>
>   *Case 2:*   Dividends.
>   *Determinant:*   Independently determined data.
>   *Dependency:*   None.
>   *Parameter:*   None (absolute value entry).

Shareholders' loans and capital type investments are funds which, although formally constituting debt or otherwise made repayable, feature characteristics of capital. They are often legally constructed on the basis of subordination to all other claims, and may thus, for the purposes of risk analysis, be considered as 'mezzanine capital', that is, capital substitutes. They are strategic inputs and are entered in the financial plan as absolute values.

> *Projection method:*
>   *Determinant:*   Independently determined data.
>   *Dependency:*   None.
>   *Parameter:*   None (absolute value entry).

Provisions

Provisions, that is, amounts set aside to meet certain expected obligations in the near future, are, for the time being, still part of shareholders' funds.

Deferred taxation is, in the main, the provision for tax already charged against net profit in the income statement but not yet due.

> *Projection method:*
>> *Determinant:* Tax as per current income statement.
>> *Dependency:* Equal to determinant.
>> *Parameter:* Equality.

Other short-term provisions such as for guarantees and other contingencies will tend to increase with business activity.

> *Projection method:*
>> *Determinant:* Total or sectoral sales revenue.
>> *Dependency:* Proportional change.
>> *Parameter:* Percentage of determinant.

Debt

BORROWINGS FROM ASSOCIATED COMPANIES

These items are listed separately from other creditors because they are usually by law or agreement subordinated to other debt and, in that case, increase the financial stability of the company. They may constitute strategic investments but also reflect current balances deriving from intra-group trading.

> *Projection method:*
>> *Case 1:* Strategic investments.
>> *Determinant:* Independently determined data.
>> *Dependency:* None.
>> *Parameter:* None (absolute value entry).

>> *Case 2:* Current intra-group trade creditors.
>> *Determinant:* Relevant sectoral sales revenue.
>> *Dependency:* Proportional change.
>> *Parameter:* Percentage of determinant.

LONG-TERM DEBT

Long-term loans such as mortgages and bonds are usually amortised by periodic repayments, often by fixed payments including an interest and a redemption component. In such cases an amortisation schedule will exist from which the periodically reducing values can be lifted or inferred.

> *Projection method:*
>> *Determinant:* Independently determined data.
>> *Dependency:* None (independently determined payment
>> schedule).
>> *Parameter:* None (absolute value entry).

Long-term provisions are items mainly found in larger companies, especially those that operate pension schemes. These will be related to the total amount of salaries. Other long-term provisions are often of the kind that does not change frequently and, for the purposes of planning, can be entered at current levels.

> *Projection method:*
> | | |
> |---|---|
> | *Case 1:* | Provision for staff pensions. |
> | *Determinant:* | Total or sectoral staff costs (salaries). |
> | *Dependency:* | Proportional change. |
> | *Parameter:* | Percentage of determinant. |
>
> | | |
> |---|---|
> | *Case 2:* | Other long-term provisions. |
> | *Determinant:* | Current value. |
> | *Dependency:* | Equal to determinant. |
> | *Parameter:* | Equality (repetition). |

Other long-term liabilities are a catchall item which, unless changes or dependencies are clearly indicated, can be projected on a no-change basis.

> *Projection method:*
> | | |
> |---|---|
> | *Determinant:* | Current value. |
> | *Dependency:* | Equal to determinant. |
> | *Parameter:* | Equality (repetition). |

CURRENT LIABILITIES

Trade creditors result from payment terms conceded by suppliers. They are conveniently expressed in terms of months.

> *Projection method:*
> | | |
> |---|---|
> | *Determinant:* | Total or relevant sectoral cost of materials, components and services (cost of sales). |
> | *Dependency:* | Multiple of the average value of the determinant over a suitable space of time (e.g. one moving quarter). |
> | *Parameter:* | Number of plan periods (e.g. months). |

Other current liabilities (other than bank advances and overdrafts), such as tax liabilities and advance payments received, may, if insignificant, be assumed to be settled during the first or the first few plan periods of the plan. Otherwise they could be made dependent on total business activity.

> *Projection method:*
> | | |
> |---|---|
> | *Determinant:* | Total sales revenue. |
> | *Dependency:* | Proportional change. |
> | *Parameter:* | Percentage of determinant. |

Bank advances and overdrafts represent the firm's short-term borrowings from banks. In principle, overdrafts are repayable on demand, although they can turn into a quasi medium-term facility under a credit line arrangement, as also the term of advances can be extended by rollover agreements. In financial plans, the item is usually the balancing statistic that makes projected total liabilities equal total assets in projections (see the technical note on page 105). If the plan projections result in consistently high levels of current bank borrowing in the planning period, this indicates a revision of the plan in favour of less expensive longer-term finance.

II. Investment and funding

Reference
code

3. Funding (liabilities)

3.1 Shareholders' funds

	Period t-1	*Period t*	
Paid up ordinary shares	500	500	*2111.*
Reserves	350	350	*2112.*
Unpaid shares	0	0	*2113.*
Other claims on shareholders	0	0	*2114.*
Shareholders' capital	**850**	**850**	***2110.***
Balance on profit and loss account c/f	-484	-337	*2121.1*
Profit or loss for the year (c/f from Plansheet 10)	647	1 527	*2121.2*
Profit and loss account before dividends	163	1 190	*2121.*
- Dividends/withdrawals	500	1 000	*2122.*
Profit and loss account	**-337**	**190**	***2120.***
Shareholders' loans	350	400	*2131.*
Preference shares, participating bonds etc.	1 000	1 000	*2132.*
Shareholders' loans and capital type investments	**1 350**	**1 400**	***2130.***
Shareholders' funds	**1 863**	**2 440**	

3.2 Provisions

	Period t-1	*Period t*	
Deferred taxation	**627**	**1 354**	***2211.***
Other short-term provisions	**41**	**81**	**2212.**
s*pecifically:*			
For product guarantees	23	56	*2212.1*
For maintenance obligations	12	18	*2212.2*
For current staff claims	6	7	*2212.3*
etc.			
Total short-term provisions	**668**	**1 435**	***2210.***

Plansheet 15

II. Investment and funding

(6 of 7)

Reference
code

3. Funding (liabilities)

3.3 Debt

	Period t-2	Period t-1	Period t	
3.3.1 Associated companies				
Loans from associates		170	200	*2221.*
Other amounts owed to associates		50	25	*2222.*
Total borrowings from associates		**220**	**225**	**2220.**
3.3.2 Long-term debt				
Long-term loans				
+ *New debt*		0	0	*2231.11*
- *Repayments*		89	86	*2231.12*
Loan 1	185	96	10	*2231.1*
+ *New debt*		500	0	*2231.21*
- *Repayments*		125	125	*2231.22*
Loan 2	1 200	1 575	1 450	2231.2
etc.				
+ *Total new debt*		500	0	*2231.01*
- *Total repayments*		214	211	*2231.02*
Total long-term loans		**1 671**	**1 460**	**2231.**
Long-term provisions				
Pensions		455	475	*2232.1*
Other		30	33	*2232.2*
Total long-term provisions		**485**	**508**	**2232.**
Other long-term liabilities		16	5	*2233.*
Total long-term debt		**2 172**	**1 973**	**2230.**

Plansheet 16

II. Investment and funding

(7 of 7)   Reference
code

3. Funding (liabilities)

3.3 Debt (continued)

	Period t-1	Period t	Reference code
3.3.3 Current liabilities			
Trade creditors	479	569	2241.
Tax liabilities (net)	34	43	2242.1
Other short-term liabilities	77	98	2242.2
Deferred charges/advances received	52	154	2242.3
Other current liabilities	163	295	2242.
Balance on current account	181	0	2243.1
Advances and other short-term facilities	68	382	2243.2
Bank advances and overdrafts	249	382	2243.
Total current liabilities	**891**	**1 246**	**2240.**

Plansheet 17

17 *Rating Your Financial Stability and Performance*

Having completed the structure of your financial planning model we can now summarise the salient results in the two-page financial statement displayed in Plansheets 1 and 2 (pages 108 and 109) with the confidence of being able to name the key factors that determine the individual dynamics as well as the interactions of each of its elements.

We are now also ready to carry out the various kinds of analysis which produce the criteria preferred by raters for assessing the financial risk of your enterprise.

Structural analysis

The simple operation of converting the series of projected financial statements into percentage terms provides the basis for comparing your situation with that of other companies in your industry in what raters term peer analysis.

The advantages of conducting your planning on a monthly basis have been emphasised before. However, short-term fluctuations and the seasonal cycle make it difficult to interpret changes in structural features between any two successive months. In order to produce meaningful signals of change it is advisable to conduct the structural analysis on the basis of 12-month moving averages, an operation your spreadsheet calculator performs with ease.

INCOME AND EXPENDITURE

The structural analysis of your income statements presents a revealing record of the cost efficiencies of your business, and its projections show how you expect these to develop. The trends and patterns that stand out in the analysis provide a first occasion for critically considering the feasibility of the plan. The assessment is facilitated if the analysis, as in the following example, is split into two parts, the first dealing with the 'variable' and the second with the 'fixed' costs of producing the planned revenue.

INVESTMENT AND FUNDING

The structural analysis of the balance sheet enables a first assessment of your firm's financial risk. According to the 'golden rule' of banking any asset ought to be funded for a term that at least matches its economic life. The listing of assets and liabilities in decreasing order of these criteria reveals instances of mismatch at a glance. A most important aspect of the assessment is the sufficiency of permanent funds, that is, the company's own means in the form of shareholders' capital or investments of a quasi-capital nature.

III.　Financial structure

(1 of 2)

Reference code

1. Income and expenditure

Itemisation compatible with the summary 'Income statement', Plansheet 1

Total revenue = 100%:

Revenue source 1 (Plansheet 3)	48%	*110.108*
Revenue source 2 (Plansheet 3)	32%	*110.208*
Revenue source 3 (Plansheet 3)	20%	*110.308*
Total revenue	**100%**	*110.008*
+/- Other revenue and adjustments (net) (Plansheet 3)	0%	*120.008*
Operating income	**100%**	*100.008*
- Cost of sales (Plansheet 3)	-57%	*210.008*
Gross operating profit	**43%**	*200.008*

Gross operating profit = 100%:

Gross operating profit	**100%**	*200.009*
Provisions for depreciation (Plansheet 4)	-9%	*310.009*
Staff costs (Plansheet 6)	-35%	*320.009*
General overheads (Plansheet 7)	-29%	*330.009*
- Total fixed operating costs	-73%	*300.009*
- Short-term provisions for liabilities (net) (Plansheet 8)	-1%	*410.009*
+ Other operating revenue (net) (Plansheet 8)	-1%	*510.009*
Net operating profit	**25%**	*500.009*
- Financial costs and revenue (net) (Plansheet 9)	0%	*600.009*
+ Extraordinary income and expenditure (net) Plansheet 10)	0%	*700.009*
Net profit before tax	**25%**	*920.009*
- Taxation (Plansheet 10)	-11%	*800.009*
Net profit/loss after tax	**14%**	*900.009*

Plansheet 18

III. Financial structure

(2 of 2)   Reference
                                                                  code

2. Investment and funding (balance sheet)

Itemisation compatible with the summary 'Balance sheet', Plansheet 2

	Period t-1	Period t	
Investment (assets)			
Tangible fixed assets (Plansheet 12)	62%	50%	*1110.109*
Intangible fixed assets (Plansheet 12)	4%	2%	*1110.209*
Investments in associated companies (Plansheet 13)	13%	8%	*1120.009*
Long-term financial investments (Plansheet 13)	3%	3%	*1131.009*
Other fixed assets (Plansheet 13)	0%	0%	*1132.009*
Fixed assets	**82%**	**63%**	***1100.009***
Stocks (Plansheet 14)	6%	10%	*1210.009*
Trade debtors (Plansheet 14)	9%	17%	*1221.009*
Other current assets (Plansheet 14)	3%	3%	*1222.009*
Cash and balances with banks (Plansheet 14)	0%	7%	*1223.009*
Working capital	12%	27%	*1220.009*
Current assets	**18%**	**37%**	***1200.009***
Total investment	**100%**	**100%**	***1000.009***
Funding (liabilities)			
Shareholders' capital (Plansheet 15)	15%	12%	*2110.009*
Profit and loss account (Plansheet 15)	-6%	3%	*2120.009*
Shareholders' loans and capital type investments (15)	23%	19%	*2130.009*
Shareholders' funds	**32%**	**34%**	***2100.009***
Provisions (Plansheet 15)	**11%**	**20%**	***2210.009***
Associated companies (Plansheet 16)	4%	3%	*2220.009*
Long-term debt (Plansheet 16)	37%	27%	*2230.009*
Trade creditors (Plansheet 17)	8%	8%	*2241.009*
Other current liabilities (Plansheet 17)	3%	4%	*2242.009*
Bank advances and overdrafts (Plansheet 17)	5%	4%	*2243.009*
Current liabilities	16%	16%	*2240.009*
Total debt	**57%**	**46%**	***2200.009***
Total funding	**100%**	**100%**	***2000.009***

Plansheet 19

Indicators of liquidity

CASH FLOW

As pointed out before, one of the central considerations in assessing a firm's credit risk is the likely future development of the cash flow. The principle of cash flow has already been explained on page 95 and its sources outlined in the flow diagram on page 96. It will become apparent that the structure of the financial plan illustrated in Panels 26 and 27 on pages 90 and 91 was designed to enable a cash flow analysis which traces its major contributory streams in appropriate detail.

The analysis following below is intended to convey a thorough understanding of the concept of cash flow and the mechanics by which it affects liquid reserves as stated in the balance sheet. It should be noted, though, that local accounting standards may specify the format of cash flow analysis for the purposes of published financial statements. The actual presentation to your bank will, of course, comply with those standards.

Cash inflow from business activity
The analysis distinguishes between cash inflows from revenue and those from other sources such as borrowings. This basic cash flow is defined as operating revenue after cash outflows in the form of cost of sales, staff costs and general overheads. If during the period these outflows have exceeded revenue, the cash flow will be negative.

Actual use of cash for payments
In the actual use made of this basic cash flow during the period two components are distinguished: one is the use of cash for operational essentials. These are payments in settlement of due obligations which management has, in principle, no option but to meet. The other is the use for payments management was not obliged to make in the period, but decided to make in its own free discretion.

Inflow of cash from funders
The change in capital and long-term borrowings is the second major part of the cash flow complementing that from revenue. In instances where repayments exceed additions, this cash flow, too, can be negative.

Disposable cash flow
The net result of the inflows and outflows detailed under the preceding headings is the disposable cash flow which, if positive, constitutes new cash the use of which management is free to decide.

LIQUID RESERVES

Change in reserves
Liquid reserves are assets that are either means of payment such as cash in hand and balances on current account with banks or other assets that can be converted into cash with a high degree of reliability and within a conveniently short period. Liquid reserves of the second kind are not only assets that have an immediate market value such as term deposits with banks, treasury bonds and listed securities. They usually also include so called self-liquidating assets such as trade debtors of good quality that are expected to be collected within a relatively short period, for instance, three months.

The true measure of a firm's liquidity is the net amount of liquid reserves, that is, liquid assets as defined above after deducting short-term liabilities, especially trade creditors and bank overdrafts. A measure of liquidity frequently used in financial analysis is by the 'current ratio', that is the ratio of current assets to current liabilities. A harsher test obtained by using current assets net of stocks is popularly known as the 'quick ratio', 'liquid ratio' or 'acid test ratio'.

In financial jargon there is no clear definition of the space of time implied by the expression 'short term'. In some instances, it may be used for claims or debt with a currency up to one year. For our present purposes the key issue is liquidity as a measure of risk. For this reason, liquidity should not imply periods exceeding three months. It stands to reason that in this definition of liquid reserves short-term liabilities such as bank overdrafts and trade creditors are included as offsets.

Composition of liquid reserves

By accounting arithmetic, the disposable cash flow will be reflected in the balance sheet as a commensurate change in net liquid reserves. However, in a firm's accounts current assets and current liabilities often undergo changes unrelated to the movement of cash. These reflect value adjustments that may become necessary from time to time for a variety of reasons, for example, in respect of debtors, stocks, provisions, deferred payments, etc. In order to relate the disposable cash flow to the changes in liquid reserves it is, therefore, necessary to specify changes resulting from such revaluations.

The above definition of liquid reserves includes components of differing quality. It is good practice, therefore, to analyse its composition and the changes in its components during the period.

In the example below the components are organised in three major sections: bank and liquid assets, other short-term claims and trade debtors, all three net of liabilities in their respective category. The sequence of the items listed implies an order of liquidity which will need to be decided in the individual case.

IV. Cash flow and liquid reserves

(1 of 4)   Reference
                                                              code

1. Cash inflow from business activity

Operating revenue (Plansheet 3)	25 882	100.
- Cost of sales (Plansheet 3)	-14 625	210.
- Staff costs (Plansheet 6)	-3 926	320.
- General overheads (Plansheet 7)	-3 276	330.
Cash inflow from operations	4 055	7110.
+ Other inflows (net)[1]	175	7120.
Cash inflow from business activity	**4 230**	**7910.**

2. Actual use of cash for payments

Net additions to tangible fixed assets[2]	949	7211.11
Net additions to intangible fixed assets[3]	43	7211.12
Net additions to fixed assets (before depreciation)	992	7211.1
Net additions to other long-term assets[4]	20	7211.2
Net additions to stocks[5]	350	7211.3
Total net additions to fixed assets and stocks	1 362	7211.
Interest payments[6]	200	7212.
Tax payments[7]	1 354	7213.
Repayment of long-term debt[8]	211	7214.
Payments for operational essentials	3 127	7210.
Dividends and capital payments[9]	1 000	7221.
Repayment of shareholders' loans & capital type investment[10]	0	7222.
Other payments[11]	11	7223.
– Actual payments	**4 138**	**7200.**
= Cash surplus/shortfall after payments	**92**	**7920.**

Notes on data sources:

[1]	7120.	= Plansheet 8: ((511.) minus (513.)) plus Plansheet 9: (620.)
[2]	7211.11	= Plansheet 11: (1111.1)
[3]	7211.12	= Plansheet 11: (1111.2)
[4]	7211.2	= Plansheet 13: Change (1130.) plus Change (1140.)
[5]	7211.3	= Plansheet 14: Change (1210.)
[6]	7212.	= Plansheet 9: (610.)
[7]	7213.	= Plansheet 10: (800.)
[8]	7214.	= Plansheet 15: (2231.02)
[9]	7221.	= Plansheet 15: Change (2110. If <0) + (2122.)
[10]	7222.	= Plansheet 15: Change (2130. If <0)
[11]	7223.	= Plansheet 16: Change: (2233. If <0)

Plansheet 20

IV. Cash flow and liquid reserves

(2 of 4)   Reference
                                                        code

3. Inflow of cash from funders

Shareholders[1]	50	7310.
Associated companies (net)[2]	135	7320.
Long-term loans and other[3]	0	7330.
Cash inflow from funders (net)	**185**	**7300.**

Notes on data sources:

[1] 7310. = Increase: Plansheet 15: (2100. if >0)
             plus change: Plansheet 15: (2130. if >0)
[2] 7320. = Change: Plansheet 13: (1120.) x (-1)
             plus change: Plansheet 16: (2220.)
[3] 7330. = Change: Plansheet 16: (2231.01)
             plus change: Plansheet 16: (2233. if >0)

4. Disposable cash flow

+ Cash surplus/shortfall after payments (c/f from Plansheet 20)	92	7920.
+ Cash inflow from funders (see above)	185	7300.
= Disposable cash flow	**277**	**7930.**

Plansheet 21

IV. Cash flow and liquid reserves

5. Change in reserves

Change in reserves by cash flow (c/f from Plansheet 21)	**277**	*7930.*
Modification of liquid reserves by book entries		
Net short-term provisions for liabilities[1]	-78	*7410.*
Net revaluation of assets other than for depreciation[2]	-102	*7420.*
Change in short-term provisions[3]	767	*7430.*
Change in long-term provisions[4]	23	*7440.*
Change in deferred charges (liabilities)[5]	102	*7450.*
Change in deferred accruals (assets)[6]	-20	*7460.*
	‾‾‾‾	
Net reduction in reserves by book entries	**692**	*7400.*
	‾‾‾‾	
Change in reserves as per balance sheet	**969**	*7940.*

Notes on data sources:

[1]	7410.	= Plansheet 8: (410.)
[2]	7420.	= Plansheet 8: (512.)
[3]	7430.	= Change: Plansheet 15: (2210.)
[4]	7440.	= Change: Plansheet 16: (2232)
[5]	7450.	= Change: Plansheet 17: (2242.3)
[6]	7460.	= Plansheet 14: (1222.3) x (-1)

Plansheet 22

IV. Cash flow and liquid reserves

(4 of 4)   Reference
                                                                       code

6. Composition of liquid reserves

	Period t-1	Period t	
Cash and balances with banks (Plansheet 14)	32	482	1223.
Change		*450*	*7611.*
+ Liquid investments (Plansheet 14)	85	134	1222.1
Change		*49*	*7612.*
- Bank advances and overdrafts (Plansheet 17)	249	382	2243.
Change		*133*	*7613.*
Bank and liquid assets (net)	**-132**	**234**	**7510.**
Change		***366***	***7610.***
Other short-term claims (Plansheet 14)	17	10	1222.2
Change		*-7*	*7621.*
- Tax liabilities (net) (Plansheet 17)	34	43	2242.1
Change		*9*	*7622.*
- Other short-term liabilities (Plansheet 17)	77	98	2242.2
Change		*21*	*7623.*
Other short-term claims (net)	**-94**	**-131**	**7520.**
Change		***-37***	***7620.***
Trade debtors (Plansheet 14)	523	1 253	1221.
Change		*730*	*7631.*
- Trade creditors (Plansheet 17)	479	569	2241.
Change		*90*	*7632.*
Trade debtors (net)	**44**	**684**	**7530.**
Change		***640***	***7630.***
Liquid reserves as per balance sheet	**-182**	**787**	**7600.**
Change (compare Plansheet 22)		***969***	***7940.***

Plansheet 23

Inputs for the rating process

PRINCIPLES OF THE RATING PROCESS

Financial ratios to tell good from bad firms

Ratio analysis is the prime testing tool of the financial analyst. It is the analysis of meaningful relations between various components of the four main categories of financial data which are income, expenditure, investment and funding. The key instruments that constitute your controlling dashboard will be a selection of such ratios.

Obviously, ratios are also the credit raters' stock-in-trade. The ratios they prefer are much the same as those which are popular with stock market analysts. The raters, of course, have a specific purpose. They want their ratios to help them distinguish between healthy firms and those heading for trouble. Much research has been invested in the endeavour to identify ratios capable, with a high degree of statistical confidence, to discriminate between two main classes of probability, the critically high and the acceptably low Probability of Default (PD) in the near term, and in the context, also help to assess the Loss Given Default (LGD) attending the critical cases.

The research has shown, that certain financial ratios do, indeed, possess such discriminatory powers. Their statistical reliability does, however, vary with the data sample from which they are derived. Differences have been found to exist, for example, between countries and industries. More significant, however, in the practical application of 'discriminant variables' are the individual features of a bank's lending portfolio that determine its particular risk profile. This is why, under the Basel II accord, banks have the option of an Internal Rating Based Approach (IRB). It affords them the possibility of using their own statistical experience to define the discriminant variables of their rating system.

The working principle of rating models

Although individual financial ratios may have the discriminant power, by themselves, to produce significant rating results, the statistical reliability of the rating is considerably improved by combining several significant discriminant variables in a rating *model* assigning each a contributory weight. The reason is that, although differently focused, they all relate to the same firm and tend to mutual corroboration. These statistical models can be constructed such as to return a credit risk score that distinguishes between healthy and problematic firms and, furthermore, differentiates between acceptable risks along a quality scale that allows the definition of rating categories such as used by most professional rating agencies.

For these reasons, most rating systems will feature well-known financial ratios as discriminant variables. They will differ, however, in the weights assigned to each in accordance with its contribution to the discriminatory power of the model. It is typical for rating models that the inclusion of additional variables beyond a certain number does not significantly enhance their discriminatory ability. Therefore, the number of variables will rarely exceed ten and may be as small as four. To the rating model the weights are 'constants', although they are, of course, not constant in reality. They will change in sympathy with changing characteristics of the database. This necessitates a continual re-estimation of the model with consequences for the selection and weighting of its component variables. There may also be separate models for different sectors of industry.

From the above it follows that it is possible to identify a set of financial ratios that fairly comprehensively describes the database from which rating systems can be expected to draw their individual mix of discriminant variables. They will typically be ratios that measure profitability, leverage, capitalisation and liquidity. The structure of financial statements in our example of a financial plan and the detail included in its analysis were designed to provide inputs for any ratio a rater may wish to use in a particular case.

Rating your prospects by the law of averages

Professional rating agencies mainly work under conditions which preclude a detailed consideration of the plausibility and feasibility of a firm's financial plan. They prefer their data to be factual which implies that it is typically out of date by as much as a year plus the time required for auditing and publishing financial statements. This makes predictive capability a vital issue in designing rating models. A rating model is expected to be able to predict, from data generated one to two years in the past, a firm's default occurring within the next two to five years with an adequate degree of accuracy.

Models that meet this demand have been designed and are operated by professional raters such as Moody's or Standard & Poor's. We shall later on discuss a popular version of such a scoring model for you to apply in a self-rating test.

The important conclusion to draw from this practice of rating by predictive model is that your credit rating and, consequently, your future access to finance, might be determined by a handful of ratios calculated from your most recently audited accounts. This might be highly unsatisfactory from your point of view.

In that case it will be vital for you to be in a position to show a trend in those ratios established in the past and, more important, a perspective of their future development based on a convincingly argued strategy.

THE ELEMENTS OF RATING MODELS

We shall conclude our worked example with a selection of financial ratios that will, in all probability, drive the scoring model your raters will apply in your case.

In rating practice a number of focal areas can be distinguished which are discussed below roughly in the order of raters' preference.

Equity gearing
Indebtedness
Liquidity
Profitability
Productivity
Terms of trade
Debt cover by income
Growth.

You will recall the emphasis placed on profitability earlier as the key indicator of risk (see pages 89ff.) and may find it surprising that profitability ranks only fourth in the above sequence. The reason for this illustrates the pitfalls of a rating method that uses single items in past financial statements, that is, single terms in a time series of historical values, as predictors of future conditions. The method works reasonably well as long as a statistic describes a fairly smooth path through time. The more volatile the data the less its predictive ability.

Profit is defined as a margin, that is, the difference between revenue and expenditure. This means that relatively small changes in either revenue or expenditure will produce a far greater relative change in the difference between them. Thus, even where profits show a healthy growth trend, the amplitude of fluctuations around the trend may be considerable. Consequently, taking an individual value from a time series as the basis of predictions can overstate or understate the trend by magnitudes that render the results generally unreliable.

Equity gearing

EQUITY RATIO

The ratio of equity to total funds employed or total assets is the most popular rating variable. It measures the amount by which the firm's assets can decrease before liabilities exceed assets and force it into bankruptcy. (In the absence of a definitive terminology, the term shareholders' equity is, for the purposes of this chapter, used interchangeably with shareholders' funds.)

Basic formula:
Shareholders' equity / total assets

Possible modifications:
1   Excluding intangible assets from the balance sheet by subtracting them from assets as well as shareholders' funds on the assumption that intangibles have little or no value at default.
2   Excluding cash, balances with banks and short-term financial investments from assets to avoid the effect of firms raising their cash balance by obtaining temporary short-term loans to present a healthier liquidity situation at reporting time.
3   Excluding land and buildings from fixed assets to eliminate the effect of sale-and-lease-back transactions on the analysis.
4   Including all or a part of quasi-equity debt with shareholders' equity.

Extended formula:
(Shareholders' equity + (part of) quasi-equity debt – intangible assets
– land and buildings) / (total assets – intangible assets – land and buildings – cash, bank
balances and short-term financial investments)

EQUITY TO DEBT RATIO

This alternative measure of equity gearing is preferred by some rating experts as predictor of default.

Formula:
Shareholders' equity / total debt

In the case of listed companies, the market value of shareholders' equity may be used instead of its book value. Thereby, the rater takes advantage of the market discounting all relevant information and expectations about the company in pricing its shares.

RETAINED EARNINGS RATIO

In statistical performance tests the ratio of retained earnings to assets has proved a highly significant contributor to the predictive ability of scoring models. Retained earnings are the total amount of profits a firm has re-invested in its business throughout its existence. The ratio clearly disadvantages young firms and start-ups that have had no chance yet to accumulate significant retentions. However, it is the statistical experience that firms with a track record of self-financing are less likely to default than others. Consequently, the inclusion of this ratio tends to improve the predictive ability of a scoring model more significantly than ratios based on current profit.

Formula:
(Capital reserves + balance on profit and loss account) / total assets

Indebtedness

Net indebtedness is the amount of a firm's short-term liabilities that is not covered by liquid assets or short-term claims. It is expressed as a percentage of total assets and is a measure of short-term gearing as well as liquidity. Low values indicate problems.

Basic formula:
(Current liabilities – cash and bank balances) / total assets

Possible modifications:
Including short-term financial investments in the definition of short-term cover for current liabilities.

Extended formula:
(Current liabilities – cash and bank balances – short-term financial investments) / total assets

Liquidity

CURRENT ASSETS RATIO

The ratio measures liquidity as net working capital, that is, the excess of current assets over current liabilities. Low or negative values signal danger. This measure needs to be interpreted with caution. The decline of a firm's turnover accompanied by a decrease in trade creditors can produce an increase in the ratio shortly before its failure.

Formula:
(Current assets – current liabilities) / total assets

The popular ratios of current assets to total assets and current assets to current liabilities have generally not proved reliable predictors of default.

CURRENT LIABILITIES RATIO

This ratio is useful as corroborating indicator complementing the current asset ratio. It measures the proportion of a firm's debt that is financed by trade creditors, bank credit and other short-term sources. A high value warns of a potentially unstable liquidity situation.

Basic formula:
Current liabilities / total debt

Possible modifications:
Excluding all or a part of quasi-equity debt from the definition of total debt, thereby widening the disparity between short-term and long-term funding.

Extended formula:
Current liabilities / (total debt – (part of) quasi-equity debt)

Profitability

RETURN ON INVESTMENT
This ratio has been discussed in some detail earlier (see pages 93ff.). Interest is added back, because it constitutes the return on borrowed funds, and so is corporate tax, because it is charged against returns earned for shareholders. The adjusted profit, that is, earnings before interest and tax (EBIT), represents the return earned on the totality of assets for the totality of funds employed. By measuring a firm's earning power per value unit of assets utilised, it is a prominent indicator of credit risk. Problem firms tend to have low values.

Basic formula:
EBIT to total assets
(Net profit + interest + tax) / total assets

Possible modifications:
Adding depreciation to the above definition of return as earnings before interest and tax (extending EBIT to EBITD) which makes the ratio impervious to differences in depreciation models and valuation policies between firms. Where circumstances and amounts warrant, a further extension to include the amortisation of other assets (EBITDA) might be considered.

Extended formula 1:
EBITD to total assets
(Net profit + interest + tax + depreciation) / total assets

Extended formula 2:
EBITDA to total assets
(Net profit + interest + tax + depreciation + amortisation of other assets) / total assets

RETURN ON SALES
We have seen that return on sales is one of the two components defining return on investment (ROI) (the other component being asset turnover) (see pages 93ff.). The ratio measures the profit margin on sales and, thereby, the total cost efficiency of operations.

Basic formula:
(Net profit + interest payable + income tax) / sales revenue

Possible modifications:
Substituting gross operating profit for net profit. This measure of the gross profit margin on sales implicitly indicates the efficiency of the direct (variable) costs incurred in producing revenue, by excluding the general (fixed) costs of the operation, specifically staff costs, depreciation and administrative overheads.

Complementary formula:
Gross operating profit / sales revenue

Productivity

ASSET TURNOVER

Asset turnover, the ratio of total assets to total sales is, next to return on sales, one of the two major elements of return on investment (ROI) identified earlier (see pages 93ff.). It measures the ability of the firm's asset portfolio to generate revenue, and high values indicate competitive strength. As a discriminant variable taken on its own the predictive power of asset turnover is difficult to generalise, because of the considerable differences in asset bases that exist between industries. However, its interaction with other variables makes its contribution to the overall discriminating power in some scoring models significant enough to include it.

Formula:
Total sales / total assets

STAFF PRODUCTIVITY

Staff productivity is an obvious contributor to a firm's operating efficiency. Taken on its own, it is not, however, a very reliable indicator of default. It has been shown, though, to improve the overall predictive ability of models in which it is included. Staff productivity may be measured on a per cost unit or a per head basis.

Formula 1:
Total sales / total staff costs

Formula 2:
Total sales / total number of staff

PRODUCTIVITY OF DEBT FINANCE

The ratio of interest to debt measures the cost efficiency of borrowed funds in a firm. Its general use is problematical because of considerable differences in borrowing requirements between industries, but it can, in certain applications, enhance the performance of the scoring model as a whole.

Formula:
Total sales / total cost of finance

Terms of trade

The terms-of-trade finance a firm obtains from its suppliers and that which it makes available to its customers has a profound influence on its financial structure and liquidity. The key variable in trade creditors and trade debtors is the average period of amounts outstanding. The period is usually measured in days.

TRADE CREDITORS TO COST OF SALES

The ratio measures the average number of days by which payments to trade creditors are delayed beyond due dates. Long and lengthening periods indicate a danger of default due to creditor action.

Formula:
Trade creditors / (cost of sales / 360)

TRADE DEBTORS TO SALES

The ratio measures the average collection period for trade debtors in days. Credit granted to customers may be a condition of a firm's business. Obviously, a large and growing claims portfolio ties up funds and suggests a lowering, on average, of the quality of the claims.

Formula:
Trade debtors / (total sales / 360)

Debt cover by cash flow

LONG-TERM DEBT COVER

The ratio measures debt cover as the number of years it would take for the current level of cash flow to repay the firm's total debt.

Basic formula:
Total debt / cash flow

Possible modifications:
Deducting advance payments received from debt. In certain industries such as building and construction advance payments are normal business practice and can be substantial. In its basic form the ratio would discriminate against firms in such industries.

Extended formula:
(Total debt – advance payments received) / cash flow

SHORT-TERM DEBT COVER

In this ratio current debt is substituted for total debt to measure a firm's ability to meet its current obligations from its cash flow.

Basic formula:
Current liabilities / cash flow

Possible modifications:

Deducting advance payments in order not to disadvantage firms where advances are normal practice and account for a significant part of current liabilities.

Extended formula:

(Current liabilities – advance payments received) / cash flow

Growth

The growth of a firm's business is generally taken as an indicator of its success. As a variable predicting the likelihood of default, however, growth tends to be ambiguous. While growth is clearly better than decline, fast growth is often obtained at the expense of financial stability. Especially in smaller business units, expansion is rarely financed entirely by cash flow and might lead to an excessive reliance on borrowed funds, especially short-term credit. Of the various measures of growth, sales growth appears to be preferred for inclusion in scoring models.

Formula:

Total sales in the current period / total sales in the previous period

V. Key rating indicators

For balance sheet items the mean of values for the present and the previous year is used

(1 of 4)

Reference
code

1. Equity gearing

Equity ratio

Shareholders' funds / total assets   32.8%   *8111.*
    (Plansheet 2: (2100.) x 100 / Plansheet 2: (1000.)

Extended version:
**(Shareholders' funds + quasi-equity debt - intangible assets
- land & buildings)
/ (total assets - intangible assets - land and buildings
- cash & bank balances - short-term financial investments)**   20.6%   *8112.*
    (Plansheet 2: (2100.) + Plansheet 2: (2220.)
    - Plansheet 2. (1110.2) - Plansheet 12. (1110.11)) x 100
    / (Plansheet 2: (1000.) - Plansheet 2. (1110.2.)
    - Plansheet 12. (1110.11) - Plansheet 2. (1223.)
    - Plansheet 14. (1222.1))

Equity to debt ratio

Shareholders' funds / total debt   64.0%   *8120.*
    (Plansheet 2: (2100.)) x 100 / Plansheet 2: (2200.)

Retained earnings ratio

(Capital reserves + balance on profit and loss account)
/ total assets   4.2%   *8130.*
    (Plansheet 15: (2112.) + Plansheet 15 (2120.)) x 100
    / Plansheet 2: (1000.)

2. Indebtedness

(Current liabilities - cash and bank balances) / total assets   12.4%   *8201.*
    (Plansheet 2: (2240.) - Plansheet 2: (1223.)) x 100
    / Plansheet 2: (1000.)

Extended version:
**(Current liabilities - cash and bank balances
- short-term financial investments) / total assets**   10.7%   *8202.*
    (Plansheet 2: (2240.) - Plansheet 2: (1223.)
    - Plansheet 14: (1222.1)) x 100 / Plansheet 2: (1000.)

Plansheet 24

V. Key rating indicators

For balance sheet items the mean of values for the present and the previous year is used

(2 of 4)		Reference code

3. Liquidity

Current assets ratio

(Current assets - current liabilities) / total assets
    (Plansheet 2: (1200.) – Plansheet 2: (2240.)) x 100
    / Plansheet 2: (1000.)
                  12.2%   *8310.*

Current liabilities ratio

Current liabilities / total debt
    Plansheet 2: (2240.) x 100 / Plansheet 2: (2200.)
                  31.8%   *8321.*

Extended version:
Current liabilities / total debt – quasi-equity debt)
    Plansheet 2: (2240.) x 100 / (Plansheet 2: (2200.)
    - Plansheet 2: (2220.))
                  34.0%   *8322.*

4. Profitability

Return on investment (ROI)

(Net profit + interest + tax) / total assets
    (Plansheet 1: (900.) + Plansheet 9: (610.)
    + Plansheet 1: (800.)) x 100/ Plansheet 2: (1000.)
                  46.9%   *8411.*

Extended version:
(Net profit + interest + tax + depreciation)
/ total assets
    (Plansheet 1: (900.) + Plansheet 9: (610.)
    + Plansheet 1: (800.) + Plansheet 1: (310.)) x 100
    / Plansheet 2: (1000.)
                  61.7%   *8412.*

Return on sales

Version 1:
(Net profit + interest + tax) / total sales
    (Plansheet 1: (900.) + Plansheet 9: (610.)
    + Plansheet 1: (800.)) x 100 / Plansheet 1: (110.)
                  11.9%   *8421.*

Version 2:
Gross operating profit / total sales
    Plansheet 1: (200.) x 100 / Plansheet 1: (110.)
                  43.3%   *8422.*

Plansheet 25

V. Key rating indicators

For balance sheet items the mean of values for the present and the previous year is used

Reference
                                                                                code

5. Productivity

Asset turnover

Total sales / total assets (number of times)   4.0   *8510.*
   Plansheet 1: (110.) / Plansheet 2: (1000.)

Staff productivity

Version 1:
Total sales / total staff costs (value per unit of costs)   6.62   *8521.*
   Plansheet 1: (110.) / Plansheet 1: (320.)

Version 2:
Total sales / total number of staff (value per head)   520   *8522.*
   Plansheet 1: (110.) / Plansheet 5: (321.)

Productivity of debt finance

Total sales / total cost of finance (value per unit of costs)   130   *8530.*
   Plansheet 1: (110.) / Plansheet 9: (610.)

6. Terms of trade

Trade creditors to cost of sales

Trade creditors / cost of sales (days)   13   *8610.*
   Plansheet 2: (2241.) / (Plansheet 1: (210.) / 360)

Trade debtors to sales

Trade debtors / total sales (days)   12   *8620.*
   Plansheet 2: (1221.) / (Plansheet 1: (110.) / 360)

Plansheet 26

V. Key rating indicators

For balance sheet items the mean of values for the present and the previous year is used

(4 of 4)		Reference code

7. Debt cover by cash flow

Long-term debt cover

Total debt / cash flow   (number of periods)   0.8   *8711.*
  Plansheet 2: (2200.) / Plansheet 20: (7910.)

Extended version:
(Total debt - advance payments received)
/ cash flow (number of periods)   0.8   *8712.*
    (Plansheet 2: (2200.) - Plansheet 14: (1222.3))
    / Plansheet 22: (7910.)

Short-term debt cover

Current liabilities / cash flow (number of periods)   0.3   *8721.*
  Plansheet 2: (2240.) / Plansheet 20: (7910.)

Extended version:
(Current liabilities - advance payments received)
/ cash flow (number of periods)   0.2   *8722.*
    (Plansheet 2: (2240.) - Plansheet 14: (1222.3))
    / Plansheet 20: (7910.)

8. Growth

Sales in current period / sales in previous period   31.6%   *8800.*
    (Plansheet 1: (110.)$_t$ - Plansheet 1: (110.)$_{t-1}$) x 100
    / Plansheet 1: (110.)$_{t-1}$

Plansheet 27

IV *Passing the Test: Step Three – Presenting Your Credentials*

18 *Conclusive Statements of Value and Risk*

The most inclusive measure of business performance is the overall yield of an enterprise (popularly, its Return on Investment or ROI). It is, therefore, a convenient indicator by which to sum up – and rate – your business from a banker's point of view. Since yield is just another way of expressing value, the same goes for prospective investors in your equity. For speaking to either with confidence you need to understand how these measures are derived, and this chapter tells you how.

With that groundwork behind you, you will be ready for a self-rating exercise. We shall use the popular Z-score method as a template for you to enter your own data. The self-test will give you a realistic impression of what to expect in an actual rating situation.

Market value as a measure of risk

There is an academic debate carried on between rating specialists as to whether a firm's profitability, that is, its ability to produce returns for its shareholders, is a suitable indicator of credit risk. As we have seen, measures of profitability rank in the middle field of preference among rating professionals, and then it is mainly the return on investment (ROI), the most inclusive concept of profitability, that is chosen.

Basel II principles, however, do not merely apply to bank credit, but equally to equity investments made by a bank or a bank-owned investment company. Equity investments, direct or indirect, voting or non-voting constitute one of the five major classes of banking-book exposure that require a risk rating (see Panel 2 on page 14). Moreover, Basel II is setting standards of risk management that will be difficult to ignore by any investment management accountable for its action to the owners of funds invested, irrespective of whether or not they are directly subject to Basel II rules. Obviously, for the financial, as distinct from the strategic, equity investor the return on equity is the prime motivator and, by the same token, the prime measure of risk.

EARNING POWER AS GENERATOR OF VALUE

> In essence, a commercial enterprise is an organisation engaged in activities intended to produce returns for its owners in the form of financial surpluses over expenditures incurred in the process.

This definition implies that the market value of an enterprise relates to its ability to generate returns for its owners, not to the proceeds that might conceivably be realised by a liquidation of its various assets. The market value of a successful concern is expected to exceed that amount by a significant margin. If its market value were to sink below the combined liquidation value of its assets, it would, at best, be a proposition for 'asset stripping'.

An exception to this concept of valuation are assets that are not essential to the firm's operation and have an independent market value, for example, unutilised property or property that might be liquidated in a sale-and-lease-back transaction. Liquidation values also enter a credit rater's evaluation of, in Basel II terms, the Loss Given Default (LGD) of an exposure to a firm's business risk.

The general acceptance of the principle that a firm's market value is determined by its profitability is evidenced by the stock markets, where it is common practice to express the relationship of price and earnings in the concept of earnings yield:

$$\text{Earnings yield (\% p.a.)} = \frac{\text{earnings per share}}{\text{share price}} \times 100$$

Whereas earnings per share are taken as given, that is, usually obtained from the firm's most recent financial statement, the price is adjusted by the market to a level that implies a yield acceptable for share investors. Arithmetically, this means that the net asset value of the firm as per its financial statements is multiplied by a factor that represents the investors' collective judgement of risk inherent in the firm's business.

The general relationship reflected in the stock exchange formula is:

$$\text{Risk adjusted return on equity (\% p.a.)} = \frac{\text{net profit after tax}}{\text{net asset value} \times \text{risk factor}} \times 100$$

The risk aspect is stressed, when investors express their evaluation of a share in terms of the price-earnings (P/E) ratio, the reciprocal of the earnings yield:

$$\text{Price-earnings ratio} = \frac{\text{share price}}{\text{earnings per share}}$$

The ratio states the number of yearly earnings at the current level investors are prepared to pay for a share.

There is an alternative way of making the risk element explicit in the relationship, and it is the one usually adopted in practice: risk may be expressed as a yield premium investors require over and above a reference rate which, for them, represents a risk-free investment, such as the yield on gilt-edged sovereign bonds.

Risk premium (%)
= return on equity as per financial statement − risk free market yield

where

$$\text{Return on equity as per financial statement (\% p.a.)} = \frac{\text{net profit after tax}}{\text{net asset value}} \times 100$$

This method is more convenient, because the three input variables, net profit after tax as per income statement, net asset value as per balance sheet and the current market yield on risk-free investments, are treated as givens. If stock market investors as a group consider the risk premium relating to a particular share as inadequate, they will not buy until the market mechanism has adjusted the price such as to offer a yield that includes an acceptable premium. By the same principle, evaluators of a firm's equity will adjust their assessment of its value such as to correspond with a risk premium they consider appropriate. Although the judgement of exactly what premium is appropriate in an individual case may be inspired by investor sentiment in the relevant market environment, it will, of necessity, largely be a personal and, consequently, highly subjective, decision.

The above considerations lead to these conclusions:

The market value of a firm's equity is created not by the market value of its assets, but by its earning power.

Arithmetically, a firm's equity value is related to its earnings by an equalising risk factor.

The risk factor is essentially determined by the subjective judgement of the evaluator.

THE VALUE OF EQUITY

There can be no doubt that a firm's sustainable earning power is the most elementary determinant of the risk borne by its funders, irrespective of whether their exposure is in the form of current credit, term loans or equity investments. For good reason the return on investment (ROI) is next to cash flow the primary focus of financial analysis (see *Focus number one: Income generation and return on investment*, pages 93ff.). In assessing the risk of an equity investment the more relevant return is that earned for shareholders, defined as ROI after interest payable to lenders. That return expressed as a percentage of the equity is the earnings yield discussed above. This emphasises the fact that value and risk of equity investment both have their roots in the firm's earning power.

As explained above, a single historical profit figure is no reliable indicator, let alone predictor, of profitability (see *The elements of ratings models*, page 149). The concept of profitability contains an element of time. It is best represented by a series of profit statistics through a time period long enough to combine them into a meaningful average or, better still, a significant trend. Profitability in those terms is a strong argument to counter an unfavourable rating based on a single profit statistic and a judgmental bias deriving not from the performance of your firm, but from a sample survey of others.

Naturally, from a lender's or investor's point of view it is not the past but the future profitability of your enterprise that counts and, naturally, too, their judgement will reflect a highly subjective element of personal conviction. In order for your profitability argument to convince, your profit projections will need to be objective which, in terms of the future, means plausible. Profits result from business activity which economic theory defines as the combination of entrepreneurship with the factors of production: land, labour and capital. The firm representing the risk-taking entrepreneurial organisation of production ensures the control of required production factors by either owning or hiring them which, in the firm's books, translates into the two major categories of assets and expenditure. Therefore, plausibility of profit projections means plausible projections of sufficiently detailed balance sheets and income statements over a period which, by general convention, should not be less than five years. Ideally, that is, if available, these projections should be presented as the extension of a historical record of financial data over a comparable period in order to demonstrate plausibility in terms of both continuity and improvement.

Whereas statements of profitability in terms of earnings yield tend to reflect the firm's most recently reported accounts, as is common stock exchange practice, the assessment of a firm's value, such as for purposes of acquisitions and mergers, is more explicitly time conscious. The fundamental principle of valuation is this:

The value of a business enterprise equals the present value of its future earnings.

Whether, for the purposes of equity valuation, earnings should include or exclude corporate tax is a matter of analytical focus, local practice or legislation. Corporate tax is a claim on profits, not a cost. In principle, it is a kind of income tax levied not on the company as such, but on its shareholders to whom those profits accrue. This would argue a valuation based on earnings *before* corporate tax. In any case, from the company's point of view, corporate tax is part of the distribution of profits earned for its shareholders. However, the market value of its shares will in practice be determined by their net yield, that is, by earnings *after* corporate tax.

Credit raters are not specifically interested in the imputed market value of your equity as a measure of risk. However, Basel II rules apply also to equity investments by banks or securities firms operating under banking supervision. In that case equity value and share price are the key subjects of risk considerations.

Generally, however, managers and executives negotiating any form of finance for their businesses should have an awareness of the market value of their firm's equity, irrespective of whether or not its shares are quoted on a stock exchange.

Putting a price on your business

There exists an extensive body of literature devoted to the principles and problems of valuing businesses as going concerns. For your practical purposes, however, no more is needed than placing your firm in an order of value to provide orientation in your dealings with bankers and raters. In fact, even a valuation by a professional assessor would not achieve significantly more than that, since the unavoidable subjective element renders all such valuations tentative, hence inconclusive for third parties.

THE PRESENT VALUE OF FUTURE EARNINGS

Arithmetically, the present value concept is simple and straightforward. It is, at core, a compound interest calculation. Earnings accruing at the end of a future year are considered as the sum of a principal capital invested at the beginning of the current year adding interest to the accumulated principal at the end of each intervening year.

The present value of future earnings

Future value assuming an accumulation of interest:

Capital at the end of the year C_1 equals the capital at the start of the year C_0 plus interest, that is, i% of that capital:

$$C_1 = C_0 + C_0 \times i\% / 100$$
$$\text{or} \quad C_1 = C_0 \times (1 + i\% / 100)$$

Earnings accruing at the end of

Year 1: $C_1 = C_0 \times (1 + r)$ where r = interest factor = $(1 + i\% / 100)$
Year 2: $C_2 = C_1 \times (1 + r)$ = $(C_0 \times (1 + r)) \times (1 + r) = C_0 \times (1 + r)^2$
Year 3: $C_3 = C_2 \times (1 + r)$ = $((C_0 \times (1 + r)) \times (1 + r)) \times (1 + r) = C_0 \times (1 + r)^3$

Year n: $C_n = C_0 \times (1 + r)^n$

Solving for present value: i% becomes the discount rate and the general formula transforms to:

$$C_0 = \frac{C_n}{(1 + i\%/100)^n}, \quad \text{where } (1 + i\% / 100) = \text{discount factor.}$$

Thus:

$$\text{Present value of profit in year n} = \frac{\text{Profit in year n}}{(1 + \text{discount rate} / 100)^{\text{number of years}}}.$$

Panel 30

Applying this simple present value formula to the projected series of net profits after tax as per your financial plan and summing the results is all that is needed to obtain a view of your firm's equity value. For that, however, values for the two other variables in the formula have to be established: the number of years and the rate of interest.

THE TIME HORIZON FOR PROFIT PROJECTIONS

If it is assumed, as it usually is, that the firm for which the profit projections have been made still exists at the end of the projection period it would be unrealistic to leave profits beyond that time horizon out of account. On the other hand, it is difficult to rationalise financial plans that extend too far into the future. By convention, a detailed plan analysis of the kind described in the preceding section is expected to cover a period of at least five years with two to three years analysed on a monthly basis. In special cases, for instance, where major investments in plant or property merit a longer-term perspective, planning horizons may extend to ten years or more.

With increasing distance from the present the uncertainty of the future increases exponentially. In certain cases it may not be unreasonable to assume that the broad aggregates of balance sheet and income statement will continue along a typical trend or development pattern, especially, where these can be shown to have been established in the historical performance record.

Profits are the net result of much larger aggregates being set off against each other and, thus, highly sensitive to marginal aberrations of those aggregates from their projected time paths. Consequently, profits are far more problematical to project than the aggregates that define them. Beyond a relatively short term, such as the conventional five-year period for detailed financial planning, profit projections for individual years will become mainly speculative. When using profit projections for purposes of equity valuation, it is, therefore, more realistic to use averages, such as moving averages describing an established trend or pattern or, failing such discernible tendencies, a conservatively estimated long-term average.

Intricate projection models have been developed aligning a firm's profit growth with environmental factors, notably business cycle indicators such as GDP and stock market yields. Inevitably though, even the more sophisticated methods are based on grossly simplistic assumptions. However, the effect of actual aberrations from long-term profit projections is significantly mitigated by the exponential increase with time of the discount which reduces future values to present values. The considerable power of the mitigating effect will be demonstrated further below by repeating the calculation of a simple valuation with varying rates of discount. By implication, the effect of increasing the sophistication of valuation method dissipates too fast to warrant major efforts. Consequently, present values of future profits can, at best, serve as plausible benchmarks. Even so, such benchmarks are indispensable as guides in arriving at a judgement of fair value, for instance, when negotiating the price of a company's shares. To place matters in perspective: the valuation method practised on stock exchanges is considerably cruder. There, the price of a company's shares is represented as a multiple of earnings reported in the most recently published accounts which implies the assumption by investors that those earnings will continue unchanged at their last recorded level.

A pragmatic way of solving the problem is the combination of both the projection of individually estimated profits through the period of detailed financial planning and the assumption of a minimum or average level beyond that period. Arithmetically, the accrual of a fixed amount at the end of each year is an annuity and, where the term of the annuity is assumed to be infinite, a perpetuity.

The present value of constant future earnings

The concept of a perpetuity:

The assumption of an annual payment P to be received in perpetuity implies that the capital C out of which the payments are made remains unchanged. This implies, in turn, that the annuity equals the yearly interest of i% earned by the capital.

$$P = C \times i / 100 .$$

Solving for present value this transforms to:

$$C = \frac{P}{i / 100} .$$

If the concept is to be applied to the future beyond a certain year n, the value of C relates to the beginning of year n+1, that is, the end of year n. Therefore, C is to be discounted to its present value over the period n. By the present value formula as per Panel 30 that value is:

$$C_0 = \frac{C}{(1 + i / 100)^n} = \frac{P}{i/100 \times (1 + i / 100)^n} .$$

Thus:

Present value of a perpetuity begin-ning in year n	=	$\dfrac{\text{Profit in year n}}{(\text{discount rate}/100) \times (1 + \text{discount rate} / 100)^{\text{number of years}}}$.

Panel 31

THE CRITICAL MEASURE OF RISK: THE RATE OF DISCOUNT

We have seen that the critical variable in equity valuations is the rate by which future earnings are discounted to their present value, since, apart from the general pattern of yields and interest rates prevailing in the market environment, it includes a premium in consideration of the specific risks of an investment in the equity concerned.

Generally, the rate of discount in equity valuations is considered an aggregate of the components included in the following example:

**The rate of discount for computing
the present value of future earnings**

Example

Market yield adjusted for inflation:

Basic ('risk free') market yield[1]	4.5 %
- Rate of inflation	2.0 %
= 'Real' market yield	2.5 %

+ Risk adjusted rate of discount:

+ Premium for general risks of the industry	8.0 %
+ Premium for special risks of the firm	12.0 %
+ Premium for restricted marketability[2]	4.0 %
= Total risk premium	24.0 %
= *Rate of discount*	26.5 %

1 e.g. on a class of gilt-edged sovereign bonds
2 e.g. in the case of non-listed companies

Table 9

VALUATION ARITHMETIC: AN EXAMPLE

The above example shows the weight of subjective judgement in valuations: the rate of discount applying to future earnings is mainly determined by risk premiums. Among these, the premium for the special risks associated with the firm evaluated is the most important. It is also the one that most explicitly reflects the opinion an investor or rater has formed about the plausibility of your profit projections.

By applying the rate of discount to projected profits the equity value of the firm is obtained as shown in Table 10.

**Estimate of equity value
as the present value of future earnings**

Example

Period in years n	Discount factor[1] $f = 1.285^n$	Net Profit before or after tax[2]	Present value (Profit / f)
1	1.2650	− 495	− 391
2	1.6002	2 351	1 469
3	2.0243	5 876	2 903
4	2.5607	6 799	2 655
5	3.2393	7 689	2 374

Present value of profits during plan period:			9 010
Expected average level of profits from year 6:		7 700	
Value of profits from year 6 at the start of year 6:		29 057	
Present value of profits from year 6:			
5	3.2393	29 057	8 970

Estimate of equity value		**17 980**

---

1 Discount rate = 26.5% (see Table 9) converted into a
   discount factor = 1 + 26.5/100 (see Panel 30)
2 As preferred (see *The value of equity*, page 165f, esp. paragraph 5)

Table 10

It is instructive to repeat the above calculations for different discount rates. As can be seen in the following table, the present value of future earnings decreases exponentially with increasing discount rates.

**The effect of the rate of discount
on the estimate of equity values**

Example using the data in Table 10

Discount rate	Equity value
10 %	63 137
20 %	26 461
30 %	15 050
40 %	9 765
50 %	6 840

Table 11

The valuation exercise forcefully drives home these points:

The value of your equity is the present value of your firm's future earnings.

The magnitude of future earnings is largely a matter of subjective assessment. It reflects the answers given by the evaluator to these two questions:
1   Are the earnings feasible in terms of opportunity, taking into account the firm's operational capacity as well as conditions in its markets and industry?
2   Is the firm's management able to realise that opportunity?

EVA: The concept of economic value added

Much research effort has been expended on improving measures of profitability for the purposes of risk assessment. One of these which has found widespread acceptance among company analysts is outlined overleaf. It has been developed by the consultants J. Stern and B. Stewart and gained popularity as EVA, short for economic value added. EVA is one among the various attempts of condensing the salient conclusions of financial analysis in one compact formula. Whatever the merits of this particular concept, going through the computations will deepen your understanding of the analytical concepts discussed in this book. They are essentially the same in any approach you are likely to encounter.

EVA defines profitability in terms of effective changes in equity value. For this purpose profits are included net of taxation and other non-operational items. The operative profit thus obtained is expressed as a percentage yield of the total amount of funds employed by the firm. The margin by which the firm's operative yield exceeds the cost of funds employed adds to the value of its equity.

The example of an EVA calculation uses data from the example of financial statement analysis in the preceding section as inputs (see the notes on the source data included in the table).

In determining the cost of funds employed, the cost of equity is calculated at a risk premium above the risk-free market rate. EVA applies to a particular historical accounting period. Comparing the derivation of equity cost with that of the valuation discount in Table 9 on page 169 you will note that EVA avoids subjective assumptions about the future such as the expected rate of inflation, special risks attending an investment in the firm's equity and the marketability of its shares. Risk premiums are included only in so far as they can be obtained from factual market data.

Regarding the cost of debt, only interest actually paid is taken into account. The definition of total debt as total funds employed (that is, the balance sheet total) minus equity funds includes items, such as provisions, on which no interest is payable. Since the return on total funds employed is adjusted for tax, a commensurate adjustment is made to account for tax deductibility of interest payments.

EVA
The economic value added concept of profitability

	% p.a.	% p.a.

Return on total funds employed   **22.3%**

ROF = EBIT x (1- (TR / 100)) x 100 / TF
where:

EBIT	= Net profit (earnings) before interest and tax*	3 081
TR	= Tax rate (%)*	47.0%
TF	= Total funds employed*	7 319

Cost of equity   **24.5%**

CE = YRF + PBR
where:

YRF	= Yield on risk free investments (% p.a.) (e.g. sovereign bonds)*	4.5%
PBR	= Premium for business risks (%) = (PGR – YRF) x PSR	20.0%

where:

PGR	= Premium for general business risks (%) (e.g. stock exchange index)*	8.0%
PSR	= Premium for special industry risks (factor) (e.g. beta factor of comparable firms on the stock exchange)*	5.7

Cost of debt   **2.0%**

CD (adjusted for tax deductibility) = IDR x (1 – (TR / 100))

where IDR =Interest on debt (%)= ID x 100 / TF		3.8%
where ID = Total interest paid on debt*		200
where TD = Total debt = TF – EQ		5 279
where EQ = Equity*)		2 040

Cost of total funds employed   **8.3%**

COF = Cost of equity + cost of debt
= CE x EQR/100 + CB x (100 – EQR) / 100
where:

EQR = oquity ratio (%) = EQ x 100 / TF		27.9%

EVA Economic value added   **14.0%**
= Return on total funds employed - Cost of total funds employed

---

* Notes on the source data:

Return on total funds employed::	EBIT	= Plansheet 10: (910.) + (610.)
	TR	= Plansheet 10: (800) x 100 / Plansheet 10: (910.)
	TF	= Plansheet 2: (2000.)
Cost of equity: (s Table 9 on page 169)	YRF	Compare Basic ('risk free') market yield
	PGR	Compare Premium for general risks of the industry
	PSR:	Compare Premium for special risks of the firm
Cost of debt:	ID	= Plansheet 10 (610.)
	EQ	= Plansheet 15: (2100.) – (2131.)

Table 12

Ready for rating yourself

THE CLASSIC OF Z-SCORE RATING

In an earlier section we have dealt at some length with rating models and their inputs (see, in particular, *The working principle of rating models*, page 148). Countless rating models have been proposed by researchers and are in use by rating professionals. A model designed by one of the pioneers of rating techniques has acquired widespread recognition: the Z-score[1] model designed by Edward I. Altman, Professor at New York University, in the 1960s and further developed since.[2]

The standard version of Altman's Z-score model consists of a weighted combination of five financial ratios discussed earlier in the section *Inputs for the rating process* on pages 148 to 155.

$$Z = 1.2\,X_1 + 1.4\,X_2 + 3.3\,X_3 + 0.6\,X_4 + 1.0\,X_5$$

where:

X_1 = Working capital / total assets
measures net liquid assets (current assets minus current liabilities) relative to firm size. Repeated operating losses tend to erode relative liquidity. (See also *Current assets ratio* on page 151 and Plansheet 25 on page 157, reference code 8310.)

X_2 = Retained earnings / total assets
measures cumulative profitability, that is, the firm's self-financing ability. Favours older over younger firms. (See also *Retained earnings* ratio on page 151 and Plansheet 24 on page 156, reference code 8130.)

X_3 = Earnings before interest and tax (EBIT) / total assets
measures the operating efficiency of the firm's assets uninfluenced by the effect of financial structure, especially that of gearing equity with debt. Usually referred to as ROA (return on assets) or ROI (return on investment). (See also *Return on investment* on page 152 and Plansheet 25 on page 157, reference code 8411.)

X_4 = Equity / debt
measures the excess of assets over debt, that is, the safety margin from the threshold of bankruptcy. In the case of publicly traded companies the market value of equity is used in order to incorporate the predictive element in investor behaviour. (See also *Equity to debt ratio* on page 150 and Plansheet 24 on page 156, reference code 8120.)

X_5 = Sales revenue / total assets
measures the ability of the firm's assets to generate sales revenue, also referred to as asset turnover. The use of the ratio as general default predictor is problematical, since it varies

---

1 Z-score is a statistical concept applied to detecting biases in sample distributions. It measures the distance in standard deviations of a sample from the mean.
2 The following exposition has been adapted, in particular, from a recent paper published on the Internet, *Revisiting Credit Scoring Models in a Basel 2 Environment,* Edward I. Altman, May 2002, Working Paper FIN-02-041, New York University, Leonard N. Stern, School of Business, www.stern.nyu.edu. Originally prepared for *Credit Rating: Methodologies, Rationale and Default Risk*, London Risk Books, 2002.

considerably between industries. For that reason, this term of the Z-score model is omitted in rating non-manufacturing firms. (See also *Asset turnover* on page 153 and Plansheet 26 on page 158, reference code 8510.)

MODELLING TO FIRM TYPE

The appropriate reservations that should guide the interpretation of indicators generated by statistical analysis have been noted earlier (see *Limitations of statistical method*, page 98). They apply equally to the results of mechanistic scoring techniques. In particular, industry-specific biases need to be heeded. Altman's model should, therefore, only be used in the context of a broader financial analysis.

Nevertheless, the rating test which requires only five items from a recent financial statement as input data is highly informative. Altman claims that, despite its 'static' nature, his model has so far proved superior in predictive accuracy to other modelling approaches. In several tests of predicting bankruptcies one and two years ahead he achieved an accuracy well in excess of 70%. Even so, it will benefit the analysis if Z-scores are calculated for several historical and plan periods to establish and project a trend.

Altman's model was originally estimated for the purpose of rating publicly traded corporations. It proved not equally applicable to private firms, because the term X_4 (equity / debt) had been estimated with market values of equity. Therefore, Altman estimated a second version of his model specifically for private firms using book values of equity.

Revised Z-score model for private firms:
$$Z' = 0.717 \, X_1 + 0.847 \, X_2 + 3.107 \, X_3 + 0.420 \, X_4 + 0.998 \, X_5$$

Apart from the higher weight for ratio X_4 (equity / debt) a comparison with the standard version shows a slightly increased weight for ratio X_3 (EBIT / total assets), while the weights for ratios X_1 (working capital / total assets) and X_2 (retained earnings / total assets) decreased and that for ratio X_5 (sales revenue / total assets) remained virtually unchanged.

The implicit assumption that the equity of private firms is to be evaluated at book value is a pragmatic solution, but hardly a realistic one. In rating an individual firm it is preferable to infer a market value for its equity by a method such as described in the preceding sections.

As mentioned earlier, the ratio X_5 (sales revenue / total assets) tends to reflect industry specifics and works best for manufacturing firms. For non-manufacturing firms, such as merchandising and service companies, asset turnover is significantly higher, because they are typically less capital intensive. Also, there are industries in which asset portfolios differ widely due to a leasing alternative to asset ownership. These considerations led Altman to yet another revision of his model from which the X_5 term was omitted. It is equally applied to publicly traded and private firms and uses book values of equity.

Revised Z-score model for non-manufacturing firms
(public and private):
$$Z'' = 6.56 \, X_1 + 3.26 \, X_2 + 6.72 \, X_3 + 1.05 \, X_4$$

In terms of relative weights it is mainly the ratio X_1 (working capital / total assets) which compensates for the contribution of the eliminated ratio X_5 (sales revenue / total assets).

INTERPRETING Z-SCORES

Altman's Z-score model was estimated on data obtained from two groups of firms, those that had gone bankrupt within two years of the period to which the input data related and those that had not. In a strict statistical sense, therefore, Altman's Z-score discriminates only between these two groups. The interpretation of individual scores is this: the higher a firm's Z-score, the less likely it is to suffer financial distress in the near term. Conversely, the lower the score, the higher its bankruptcy potential.

In order to discriminate more sharply between the two groups, two threshold values of Z were estimated for each of the three models, a higher and a lower 'cut-off point', leaving a 'zone of ignorance' between them. Thus, for rating purposes, the models distinguish three categories. Their specific purpose, however, is one-dimensional: it is the assessment of a firm's bankruptcy potential. In this, the models have been singularly successful. In extensive tests, the original version applied to publicly traded companies achieved accuracies in one-year predictions of bankruptcy above 80%, on average, and, in some tests, above 90%. Over the two-year term the predictive accuracy was, on average, still better than 70%.

Clearly, for rating purposes, a more differentiated interpretation of Z-scores would be preferable, at least, in terms equivalent to conventional rating categories. Altman's paper includes the results of research linking Z-scores with bond rating categories in Standard & Poor's notation.

Bond rating equivalents of Z-scores

S&P Bond Rating 1995 – 1999	Average Z-Score
AAA	5.02
AA	4.30
A	3.60
BBB	2.78
BB	2.45
B	1.67
CCC	0.95

Table 13

However, the statistical measures of reliability by category that were included in the test showed considerable variations. The tabled correspondences must therefore be considered as tentative with no practical significance attaching to the second digit after the decimal point.

Z-SCORING YOUR FIRM

The worked example of a Z-score rating that follows is intended to provide you with an easy-to-apply method for a self-rating exercise. Enough has been said about the appropriate provisos and caveats that need to be heeded in applying the method and interpreting the results, especially those concerning digital significance.

In the context of Basel II, Altman's Z-score model has enjoyed increasing popularity among bankers and raters. So, for instance, the lower cut-off point for the standard model of 1.81

is frequently referred to in publications in the sense of a benchmark. Whatever the true significance of the Z-score obtained for your firm, it helps to be aware of benchmarks that have the potential of developing into quasi-standards in credit rating.

For the purpose of illustration the same input data has been used in each of the three models. It consists of ratios resulting from the financial analysis exercise in the preceding chapter as indicated by the source references. In all three models the Z-score for the data sample is well above the upper cut-off point indicating a satisfactory state of financial health.

Z-score analysis

Sample calculations

Model Variables		Source Data			Z public firms		Z' private firms		Z" non-manufacturing	
		Plan table & page	Data code	Ratio	Weight	Weighted Ratio	Weight	Weighted Ratio	Weight	Weighted Ratio
$X_1 =$ working capital / total assets .		25 157	8310.	0.122	1.2	0.15	0.717	0.09	6.56	0.80
$X_2 =$ retained earnings / total assets .		24 156	8130.	0.042	1.4	0.06	0.847	0.04	3.26	0.14
$X_3 =$ EBIT / total assets .		25 157	8411.	0.469	3.3	1.55	3.107	1.46	6.72	3.15
$X_4 =$ book value equity / total debt .		24 156	8120.	0.640			0.420	0.27	1.05	0.67
$X_4 =$ market value equity * / total debt .				0.960	0.6	0.58				
$X_5 =$ sales revenue / total assets .		26 158	8510.	4.000	1.0	4.00	0.998	3.99		
Z-score:						6.33		5.84		4.76
Upper cut-off point: Healthy above this level						2.99		2.90		2.60
Lower cut-off point: Distressed below this level						1.81		1.23		1.10

* The market value equity is assumed to be 1.5 times its book value

Table 14

19 *Financial Competence and Risk Control*

The financial structure of an enterprise – especially the 'gearing' of equity with debt – is a potent factor determining the yield earned for its shareholders as well as the risk borne by its funders in general. For bankers and raters the design of the proposed financial structure, that is, the reasoned balancing of yield against risk, will be considered a key measure of your managerial competence. This chapter guides you in presenting an optimised financial structure in your plan.

Financial structure and financial risk

If a firm's balance sheet is highly revealing of the financial competence of its management, this is even more true for plan balance sheets which are statements of strategic intent.

In several places in the book we have had occasion to note the importance of the proportional contribution made by equity to the totality of funds employed in financing a firm's assets. Equity is the buffer absorbing a decrease in assets in phases of slow business or economic downturns. But the principle at issue here is a more general one of which the adequacy of equity is only a special case.

> It is a categorical imperative of financing that an asset must be funded by means available for a term which covers its economic life.
>
> The principle also known as 'the golden rule of banking' applies with equal emphasis to corporate finance. Any breach of this rule enhances a firm's probability of default.

Current financial statements submitted to banks in support of applications for finance typically show term disparities between assets and liabilities. They are often the very reason for making the application. Obviously, however, your banker will expect the projected balance sheets in your financial plan to show an early return to term equivalence in financing your asset portfolio. Testing the soundness of the intended financial structure of your firm is very possibly the first item in the banker's critical review of your plan. A structural analysis of investment and funding such as that illustrated in Plansheet 19 on page 141 serves to make your policy explicit in this respect.

Specifying your financial requirements

Because of its importance in containing business risk, a suitable financial structure will be a prominent goal of your strategy. Structural considerations will guide you in specifying and arguing your financial requirements.

The following case study illustrates the principles of financial structuring in the practical context of a firm requiring additional finance in consequence of rapid growth.

We assume the case of a medium-sized manufacturer of machine tools. Due to favourable market conditions turnover has increased faster than expected and necessitated new investments in plant and equipment and higher levels of stocks. These were partly financed by a mortgage on the firm's property; mainly, however, by bank credit and trade creditors.

Financial structure: A sample case
1. Starting situation

Investment (Assets)	'000	%	Funding (Liabilities)	'000	%
Land + buildings	1 200	23%	Capital	1 000	20%
Plant + equipment	2 800	55%	P&L acct.+ reserves	150	3%
Fixed assets	**4 000**	**78%**	**Equity**	**1 150**	**23%**
			Long-term loan	**700**	**13%**
Stocks	900	18%			
Debtors etc.	200	4%	Bank	2 100	41%
			Creditors etc.	1 150	23%
Current assets	**1 100**	**22%**	**Current liabilities**	**3 250**	**64%**
Total investment	**5 100**	**100%**	**Total funding**	**5 100**	**100%**

Table 15

The firm has built competitive advantage through innovative technology, and its prospects of continued sales growth are rated excellent. Management reckons that, in order fully to exploit their firm's market potential and competitive advantage, they need to invest another 1.2 million in plant and stocks.

The firm's bankers, however, are concerned over the decrease of the equity ratio to 23%, a level significantly below the 30% considered adequate by industry standards. More relevant, though, is the ongoing erosion of the relative contribution of long-term means to financing the firm's assets. By now, equity and long-term loans (together 36%) cover less than half of the fixed assets (78%). The remainder (42%) is almost entirely financed by bank facilities (41%), mainly on overdraft terms. The term discrepancy is actually worse than showing up in the condensed balance sheet, since a minimum level of stocks must be considered a long-term investment. A worrying conclusion is that firm has begun to finance long-term assets with trade creditors.

In fact, the firm has reached the limit of its borrowing capacity. Its property does not support more long-term finance than has already been raised on it. To make the bank countenance the upward drift of the firm's overdraft the owner-managers had to pledge their private residential properties as collateral. But the bankers consider that leeway to have meanwhile been exhausted and see no further latitude for increasing their exposure. For the firm's management the implications are clear: if they do not find the 1.2 million soon, they will not be able to defend, let alone further expand, their newly established market position – with foreseeable consequences. Their very success in a highly competitive environment denies them the option of retreat. Their dilemma is summarised in Table 16 which includes the required additions to the firm's asset portfolio.

Financial structure: A sample case
2. New financing requirements

Investment (Assets)	'000	%	Funding (Liabilities)	'000	%
Land + buildings	1 400	22%	Capital	1 000	16%
Plant + equipment	3 400	54%	P&L acct.+ reserves	150	2%
Fixed assets	**4 800**	**76%**	**Equity**	**1 150**	**18%**
			Long-term loan	700	11%
Stocks	1 200	19%			
Debtors etc.	300	5%	Bank	2 100	34%
			Creditors etc.	1 150	18%
Current assets	**1 500**	**24%**	**Current liabilities**	**3 250**	**52%**
			New finance required	**1 200**	**19%**
Total investment	**6,300**	**100%**	**Total funding**	**6 300**	**100%**

Table 16

The situation described here is fairly common for medium-sized firms that implement a growth strategy which competently enough deals with the vital prerequisites of marketing, production and distribution, but fails to address the financial implications on the assumption that success will attract the required additional funds in good time. Often enough, this classic mistake drives firms into an untimely sell-out, if it does not simply stop them dead in their tracks.

Obviously in this case, a lack of credit is not the problem. Quite probably, the bankers have already stretched the rules to support their client to the extent they have. Whatever other finance the firm requires, what it needs most of all is more equity. Due to the high expenditure that primed the firm's recent sales boom, profit retentions have only just begun to make contributions to equity and cannot be expected to create sufficient self-financing capacity to meet the anticipated near-term requirement of additional funds. In fact, the costs of the proposed new expansionary drive are expected to produce losses during the first two years.

At this juncture, the firm's most important asset is an immaterial one: its prospects of success, solidly based on a competitive advantage which, provided the new investment plan can be implemented, is expected to be sustained long enough to establish and fortify a position of dominance in its target market. Made communicable by an articulate business plan the prospects prove attractive for equity investors. Acting as advisor the bank offers to mediate, and contact is made with an investment unit in its group.

Upon due diligence the investment company is prepared to entertain a share offer based on a net asset or equity value of 2 250 000. The valuation is based on the assumption that the proposed investment of 1.2 million into additional productive capacity will be made as scheduled. There is the proviso that, as a matter of corporate policy, the investment company will only consider a minority share, preferably not exceeding 40%. The parties agree on the following plan. The firm issues new shares in a nominal value of 670 000, that is, 40% of the increased share capital of 1 670 000, which the investment company will buy at a price that matches the equity value of 2 250 000, that is, 900 000 (rounding the calculation (2 250 000 / 1 670 000) × 670 000). The premium of 230 000 over the nominal value will be added to reserves. The plan is summarised in Table 17.

Financial structure: A sample case
3. Capital issue

Investment (Assets)	'000	%	Funding (Liabilities)	'000	%
Land + buildings	1 400	22%	Capital	1 670	26%
Plant + equipment	3 400	54%	P&L acct.+ reserves	380	6%
Fixed assets	**4 800**	**76%**	**Equity**	**2 050**	**32%**
			Long-term loan	**700**	**11%**
Stocks	1 200	19%			
Debtors etc.	300	5%	Bank	2 100	34%
			Creditors etc.	1 150	18%
Current assets	**1 500**	**24%**	**Current liabilities**	**3 250**	**52%**
			Residual requirement	**300**	**5%**
Total investment	**6 300**	**100%**	**Total funding**	**6 300**	**100%**

Table 17

Although the share issue will leave the firm short of 300 000 for funding its investment plan, it meets one important objective: even assuming an increase in debt to cover the shortfall, it will raise the equity ratio to 32% which is within the industry norm. More than the share issue is required, however, to eliminate the serious term discrepancies between assets and liabilities not directly solved by it. Therefore, the investment company will consider the share deal only in the context of a complete restructuring of the firm's finances which they offer to assist. The guiding principles of the new planning effort are these:

The firm's fixed assets and minimum stock levels are to be financed by long-term funds.

Current bank credit such as overdrafts are to be used only to finance self-liquidating assets such as trade debtors and fast moving stocks.

Creditors include hidden financing costs evident in rebates offered against spot payment. In this case, too, bank credit proves the less expensive alternative.

In consultation with the bank the parties arrive at a final plan by which the investment company arranges for a term loan of 2 100 000 with a currency of ten years and periodical repayments beginning after the second year.

Financial structure: A sample case
4. Final financing plan

Investment (Assets)	'000	%	Funding (Liabilities)	'000	%
Land + buildings	1 400	22%	Capital	1 670	26%
Plant + equipment	3 400	54%	P&L acct.+ reserves	380	6%
Fixed assets	**4 800**	**76%**	**Equity**	**2 050**	**32%**
			Long-term loan	800	13%
Stocks	1 200	19%	New Long-term loan	2 100	33%
Debtors etc.	300	5%	**Long-term loans**	**2 900**	**46%**
Current assets	**1 500**	**24%**			
			Bank	900	14%
			Creditors etc.	450	7%
			Current liabilities	**1 350**	**21%**
Total investment	**6 300**	**100%**	**Total funding**	**6 300**	**100%**

Table 18

Including the increase in mortgage finance for the new extensions to buildings, long-term funds now amount to 78% of total assets covering fixed assets plus part of the stocks. Bank credit is used only for financing self-liquidating assets and has replaced expensive trade creditors.

Profitability

In our sample case it was mentioned that profits are not expected to make any significant contribution to the firm's self-financing capacity in the near future. In fact, the current costs of implementing the investment plan were budgeted to exceed revenue during the first two years.

Considering that profits are the prime motivator of investment, those losses might be expected to deter investors. This is not necessarily so, however. The extraneous expenditure associated with the implementation of a major expansion project may be thought of as an investment in opportunity, an immaterial asset to be written off in the period in which it is made. Naturally, start-ups, also in the sense of major new projects entered by established firms, are fraught with special risks. These will be reflected in the special risk premium investors will include in their evaluation of the firm's shares (see Table 9 on page 169). Investors who take a long-term view of a firm's profit potential might wish to take advantage of shares that appear undervalued in that perspective. In particular, venture capital investors specialise in taking advantage of such opportunities. This investment behaviour has given rise to an illustrative device, the 'hockey stick curve'.

Equity financing
Preferred entry and exit points

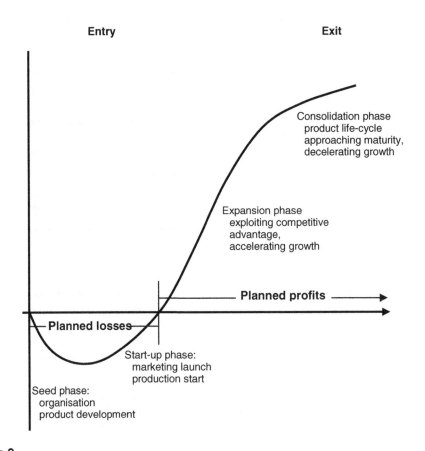

Entry   Exit

Consolidation phase
product life-cycle
approaching maturity,
decelerating growth

Expansion phase
exploiting competitive
advantage,
accelerating growth

Planned profits ──────►

Planned losses

Start-up phase:
marketing launch
production start

Seed phase:
organisation
product development

Figure 9

The concept demonstrates once again that, although profitability is the ultimate measure of success and risk, a profit statistic relating to a single period is not necessarily representative of a firm's profit potential and, hence, not a reliable indicator of risk, let alone an accurate predictor of default.

One conclusion is that it makes no sense in business plans to be shy of showing losses or reduced overall returns in the early phases of investment projects. It is rare for major projects to generate profits in the first year of their implementation. Several years may be required for the newly created profit potential to be fully realised. It is important, though, for business plans to extend far enough into the future to indicate the break-even point and include enough of the profit development beyond it for the reader to appreciate the full impact of the project on the firm's profitability. The critical item in investment analysis, as in risk analysis, is the average level of profit expected to be sustained over the long term.

Leveraging your equity yield

The return on investment (ROI) is produced by the totality of assets and, consequently, for the totality of funds that finance them. While the operational use of funds makes no distinction between equity and debt, the distribution of the proceeds between the two categories differs significantly: out of the jointly earned return, debt funds receive a predetermined interest, while equity funds take whatever remains. If the proportion of earnings relating to borrowed funds exceeds the interest, the surplus accrues to the equity which, thus, receives more that its proportional share of earnings.

The diagram illustrates the 'leverage effect' produced by 'gearing' equity with borrowed funds.

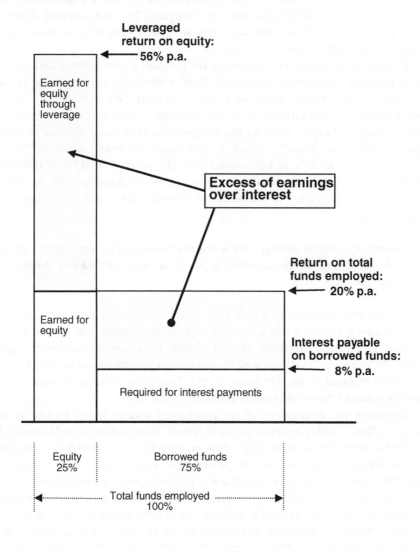

Capital gearing and leverage effect
an example

Leveraged
return on equity:
← 56% p.a.

Earned for
equity
through
leverage

Excess of earnings
over interest

Return on total
funds employed:
← 20% p.a.

Earned for
equity

Interest payable
on borrowed funds:
← 8% p.a.

Required for interest payments

Equity
25%

Borrowed funds
75%

◄············· Total funds employed ·············►
100%

Figure 10

Other conditions remaining unchanged, the return earned for equity is the higher the higher the relative contribution of debt to total funds employed. The parameters chosen to demonstrate the effect, that is, the ratio of equity to total assets (25%), the rate of interest payable on borrowed funds (8% per annum) and the rate of return on total funds employed (20% per annum) are not extreme, although, at first glance, the resulting return on equity (56% per annum) may appear so. Equity yields of that order may not be the standard, but they are not unrealistic either, especially not in the case of small to medium-sized enterprises in the expansion phase. In the final analysis it is the yield investors deem appropriate that determines the equity value at which the market prices a firm's shares. The important consequence is this:

> In business, borrowing is not a substitute for equity, but an important instrument of generating attractive returns on equity.

Obviously, the leverage effect also operates in the reverse: if total earnings fall below the interest payable on debt, the deficit is borne by the equity. This high potential of risk explains the common preoccupation of analysts and raters with the equity ratio. It adds relevance to the question of what a firm's equity ratio should be.

Essentially, the equity ratio expresses the trade-off between return and risk. Benchmarks for what might be considered a reasonably 'safe' equity ratio may be found in industry data. They differ widely between sectors of economic activity. We have already encountered one important reason for such differences: by the principle of term equivalence between assets and liabilities, a degree of capital intensity that is typical for an industry will tend to correspond with a typical equity ratio. Broadly typical in this sense are equity ratios of 30% to 40% in manufacturing, 15% to 20% in the distributive trade and 10% to 15% in the services sector. (Incidentally, what Basel II is specifically about is capital adequacy in the banking sector with the aim, stated in paragraph 5 of the document, to ensure an overall equity ratio of 8% on risk weighted assets.)

> Competent financial management will aim to minimise the contribution of equity to total funds employed while maintaining it on a level considered prudent by industry experience.

The leverage effect places a policy of self-financing in perspective. Since earnings yields required by equity investors will always be significantly higher than interest rates payable on debt, equity is the most expensive form of finance for a firm. Consequently, equity funds in excess of the minimum level indicated by risk considerations should preferably be paid out in dividends and replaced by suitable forms of debt. Such policy will, at the same time, ensure that the yield potential of the retained equity is realised to the full.

Exploiting the leverage effect for maximising returns is not merely an option but a necessity for firms wishing to attract equity investors. True venture capital investors in particular will expect to earn five to seven times their investment over a period between three and five years. Calculated on a compound interest basis this implies an average yearly rate of return between 50% and 60%. We have seen that it is perfectly possible for efficiently structured firms to realise average equity yields of that order. Even higher yields are possible in the phase of accelerating growth that typically follows the implementation of a strategy exploiting competitive advantage. Sustained profitability of the obligor firm is an important mitigant of credit and investment risk. Bankers and raters will want to be assured, however, that the optimisation of a firm's financial structure under considerations of equity yield does not create additional risks.

You will find the financial structure projected in your business plan to be judged by three major criteria:

Maximising returns: The systematic gearing of equity with debt funds maximises obtainable equity yields through the leverage effect.

Minimising risk: An adequate relation of equity to total funds employed enables the firm to absorb unforeseeable losses.

Maintaining liquidity: The availability of funds for terms that match the life of the assets financed ensures the firm's continued solvency.

To sum up:

Creating and maintaining an optimised financial structure is an elementary function of management.

Awareness of the importance of structural conditions as evidenced, for instance, in business plans is a major criterion in rating the financial competence of management.

PART V

Appendix:
A Document for
All Occasions

Stating Your Case: The Business Plan

A formal business plan or prospectus is the basis of all communications with bankers and investors. Various degrees of condensation may suit particular stages of negotiation, but your credentials rest with your ability to present an exhaustive documentation of your case. Here you find a sample prospectus with its contents referenced to items of strategic and financial planning discussed earlier as well as two typical examples of condensation into the format of an 'exposé' and an 'executive overview'.

The importance of a well-structured business plan as a means of communicating with funders, investors and raters cannot be overemphasised. The business plan or suitably condensed versions of it, are often the medium of the first contact.

It is not generally realised that the majority of business plans that are rejected by bankers and investors at first contact do not fail because the firms and projects introduced by them have no merit, but because their content is largely irrelevant, hence signals managerial incompetence. As market wisdom has it:

> You can make a first impression only once.
>
> Second chances are hard to come by.

The business plan is the medium intended to 'sell' your firm. Consequently, its design warrants at least the care and effort expended on any of the firm's major marketing campaigns. For the same reason it should reflect your own style, not some template. The sample structure of a business plan outlined below is intended as a guide, not as a recommendation.

For general guidance regarding the line of argument to be pursued by your business plan you may find it helpful to refer back to *Part II Passing the Test: Step One – Defining Your Business Strategy, Chapter 6: The Task Outlined* page 33, and, especially, two figures: *The root sources of business success*, page 34, and *Logic and scope of the rating process*, page 36.

Here also is some advice drawn from long experience as reader of business plans:

> A business plan should be sober, to the point and unambiguous. It should be free of superlatives and advertising slogans. The mode of presentation should serve to make the contents easy to absorb and avoid graphical design that does not serve that overriding purpose.
>
> A comprehensive analysis of historical and projected financial performance is an important adjunct to a business plan. However, only a few carefully selected extracts should be included in the business plan itself. The full statistical survey of historical and projected financial data should be presented in a separate document.

Descriptions of products and technical processes should be used with utmost circumspection, since the readers of business plans often lack the competence or confidence to interpret them. Selected items that are considered indispensable ought to be attached in an appendix. (In this context, the caveats expressed above in *Product strategy vs market strategy*, page 44, should be taken into consideration.)

Pictures are not always worth a thousand words. In business plans they more often distract than inform. They should be included only for a truly valid reason.

Similarly, graphical presentations of financial data are, in most instances, superfluous and a waste of space. They can, in fact, be counter-productive, if the scaling makes them difficult to interpret or creates a misleading impression.

Headings and sub-headings provide orientation, but over-structuring can have the opposite effect. For the same reason, the numbering of headings should be used judiciously, if at all. (In the sample structure of a business plan following below major headings are numbered merely to facilitate cross-references from the subsequent sections of this chapter.)

The conventional view of bankers and investors that a business plan should not exceed a volume of 30 pages is, of course, no hard and fast rule. It does, however, reflect the experience that the attention span of a reader of business plans tends to become stretched beyond that length. As a rule, a business plan that cannot be fast-read in 20 to 30 minutes is bound to lower the retention of salient information and, hence, to irritate. Concision in preparing business plans is an important factor in creating a favourable first impression with bankers and raters, especially if combined with a structure and layout designed to maximise reading speed and absorption rate.

There may be occasions that do not call for the full-report version of your business plan to be presented right away and are more effectively met by a shorter preliminary version designed to stimulate a wish for more information. A business plan proves its value especially if conceived as a master document that is continually updated and, thus, always ready at a moment's notice to be adapted to any particular use. Such ad hoc adaptation is facilitated by a structure that lends itself to various degrees of condensation. The sample structure of a business plan outlined below is followed by two examples of shortened formats, the exposé and the executive overview, which demonstrate that facility.

Contents of a comprehensive business plan

The volume indications assume a target limit for the document of 30 pages.

Statistical appendix: Survey and analysis of financial data

1. Executive summary

Concise statement of main conclusions drawn from the presentation following in the main body of the business plan. Ideally not exceeding one page.

1.1 THE FIRM

Legal entity: Name, registered office, directors, chief executive officer, management, group affiliations, major shareholders, issued capital. (See opposite *2.1 The firm and its shareholders* and *2.2 Management and organisation.*)

1.2 THE CORPORATE MISSION

Policy goals, target markets, product attributes, essential technologies, synergetic linkages, distinctive competences and resources. (See *3.3 Strategic targets, The corporate mission.*)

1.3 MAJOR FINANCIAL TARGETS AND RETURN ON CAPITAL

A small selection of plan statistics leading up to the projected returns on capital. The source of the data is the financial survey attached to the business plan in a separate appendix. Its content is described later under *Statistical appendix: Survey and analysis of financial* data, page 197. Only key information needs to be included in the main report, as suggested in *4.2 Planned financial performance*, page 195. The selection to be included under this present heading should include the last year of historical accounts and five plan years. In the interest of readability, figure notation should be confined to significant digits.

> **Heads of tabulated financial targets**
> A sample selection
>
> Equity
> Debt
> ———————————————
> Total funds employed = total assets
> *Equity ratio (%)*
>
> Sales revenue
>
> Number of employees
>
> Profit before interest and tax
> *Return on sales (%)*
>
> **Return on assets** *(%)*
> (= Return on investment ROI)
>
> Profit before tax
> **Return on equity** *(%)*

1.4 REQUIREMENT OF RESOURCES AND NEW FINANCE SOUGHT

Concise listing of additional resources required for implementing the firm's strategy and the type and amount of the finance sought for the purpose. (See page 194 *3.3 Strategic targets, Strategic action plan.*)

2. Corporate identity

2.1 THE FIRM AND ITS SHAREHOLDERS

Exhaustive listing of all information defining the firm as legal entity: Full name, company registration, registered office, physical address, directors, chief executive officer. Share capital: authorised, issued, paid-up, number and denomination of shares, planned share issues, group affiliations/major shareholders (if suitable, diagram of group structure).

2.2 MANAGEMENT AND ORGANISATION

The personalities of the executive team: name, age, qualifications, occupational career. Time with the firm, present executive responsibilities. Of particular interest: qualifications and practical experience relevant to the present function. The firm's major operational functions and processes, preferably summarised in an organisation chart identifying the areas of responsibility of the executives introduced by name.

2.3 HISTORY OF THE FIRM AND ITS BUSINESS

Ideas and plans that originated the firm, the role of founders/initiators, major stages of development up to the present. The main purpose of the information is to identify the circumstances that shaped the present situation as background to the business plan. In this sense, also start-ups have a relevant history.

3. Success potential and strategy

3.1 MARKET POTENTIAL

For general guidance refer to *Market potential*, page 49.

☐ Target markets and demand
   See *From customer needs to target markets*, page 49.
   • Target groups and unmet customer needs
   • Demand and prices
   • Environmental influences on demand
   • Special features of the target markets

☐ Success conditions for suppliers
   See *General success conditions for suppliers*, page 52.
   • Critical conditions of market success
   • Means of controlling sales volume

☐ Special competences of the firm
   See *Success conditions specific to your firm*, page 56.
   • The firm's ability to meet customer demand
   • The success profile of the firm

3.2 COMPETITIVE STRENGTH

For general guidance refer to *Competitive strength*, page 58.

☐ Industry and supply conditions
   See *Industry and supply conditions*, page 58.
   - Market potentials attracting suppliers
   - Profile of the supplier industry
   - Environmental influences on supply conditions
   - Special features of the supplier industry

☐ Strengths and strategies of competitors
   See *Strengths and strategies of competitors*, page 62.
   - Competitive conditions
   - Strategic competitor groups
   - Special features of competition

☐ Special competitive strengths of the firm
   See *The relative competitive strength of your firm*, page 65.
   - The firm's relative competitive strength
   - Conclusions of strengths and weaknesses analysis

3.3. STRATEGIC TARGETS

For general guidance refer to *Strategic Consequences*, page 69.

☐ The corporate mission
   See *Goals of corporate policy*, page 70, *The corporate mission*, page 71.
   - General (long-term) policy goals
   - Customer needs addressed
   - Product attributes
   - Target markets
   - Essential operational technologies
   - Synergetic linkages
   - Distinctive competences and resources

☐ Product information
   Refer to the discussion *Product strategy vs market strategy*, page 44.

The description of business activity, type and uses of the products and/or services marketed should avoid technical jargon.

If the product lends itself to visual presentation, a sample may be shown here (preferably on one page, avoiding a 'picture book' impression). A selection of informative product brochures (not too many, not too voluminous, not too technical) may be attached in an appendix and referenced here.

☐ Main strategic thrusts
See *Strategic thrusts*, page 71.
- Growth strategy
- Competitive strategy
- Strategic investments

☐ Strategic action plan
See *Your plan of strategic action*, page 74.
- The scope for strategic action and key result areas
- The firm's strategic strengths and weaknesses
- Requirement of resources and action plan

4. Financial plan

4.1 FINANCIAL IMPLICATIONS OF STRATEGIC TARGETS

In the business plan the discussion will selectively focus on the financial implications of the major strategic targets, e.g. within the frame of reference outlined in *Your plan of strategic action*, page 74.

☐ Income generation
- Marketing and distribution
- Products and product development
- Operational organisation and processes

☐ Resources
- Production
- Supplies
- Personnel
- Finance

4.2 PLANNED FINANCIAL PERFORMANCE

It is assumed that the financial plan is presented in a separate analysis that may, if considered suitable, be attached to the business plan as an appendix, but may also be used as an independent document. For general guidance see *Performing the projections*, page 106.

The business plan will be expected to present the main features of income statements and balance sheets. The most efficient way of doing that is to include extracts from the financial plan in a manner that facilitates a referencing of the quotes to their source.

For example, the plan data included could consist of the following five tables. If it improves the clarity of presentation, these may be condensed by aggregating sub-components, but one format for income statement and balance sheet, respectively, should be used throughout.

☐ Financial plan summary
- Income statement, *Plansheet 1*, page 108
- Balance sheet, *Plansheet 2*, page 109
- Structure of income statement (%), *Plansheet 18*, page 140

- Structure of balance sheet (%), *Plansheet 19*, page 141
- Cash flow, *Plansheets 20 and 21*, pages 144 and 145, condensed into one page

☐ Key rating indicators
Optionally, a small selection of ratio indicators might be included, for example the four (or five) components of the Z-score formula together with the resulting score (see *Z-scoring your firm*, page 175).

4.3 COMMENTS ON MAJOR FEATURES OF THE FINANCIAL PLAN

Usually, business plans submitted to banks in support of an application for finance aim to accomplish an improvement, in terms of liquidity, productivity, profitability, financial structure etc. These will be reflected as noticeable changes in the pattern of the projected data, some as discrete steps of magnitude, others as changes or reversals of trends. There may also be features which, viewed in isolation, might be considered unfavourable but are rationalised in a broader context of planned performance. A prominent example are losses due to exceptional costs and operational bottlenecks in the early phases of implementing major expansion or investment projects. These planned temporary deviations from accepted norms require exhaustive comment.

The following is a selection of sections in the financial plan which frequently call for explanatory comment. In some instances, quotes of relevant ratio indicators from the financial plan (see *Plansheets 24 to 27*, pages 156 to 159) might help to illustrate points made in the comments.

☐ Sales and operating results
The measure of business success is the return on capital. The chief parameter determining returns is revenue. Therefore, major changes in the projected sales trend naturally focus the attention of the reader.

☐ Profitability
Both the firm's total earning power as expressed in return on investment (ROI) and the return earned for equity are obvious points of interest. In particular, projected losses such as attending the implementation of major investment or marketing projects require explicit explanation.

☐ Investments
The investment in productive assets is often the main reason for a share issue or the application for a major loan. Because of their size and long-term nature such investments create important new risks for the firm and its funders. In that case a summary of the planned investments will be a prominent feature of the business plan.

☐ Employment
Human capital is the most critical resource of an enterprise. Staff often contributes the major part of a firm's current expenditure. Staff costs are 'fixed' in that they do not flexibly adjust to reductions in business activity. Staff productivity is, therefore, a major focus of risk assessment.

☐ Financing
One important goal of financial planning is to optimise the firm's financial structure. Capital adequacy and general term equivalence between assets and liabilities are prime instruments of risk control. Moreover, the gearing of equity with debt finance and the resulting leverage effect is a key determinant of the yield on shareholders' funds.

☐ Dividends
Not only to satisfy shareholder and investor preferences, but also as a means of maintaining an optimal relation between equity and debt, dividends are an important item of the business plan and should be commented on with reference to the firm's dividend policy.

Statistical appendix: Survey and analysis of financial data

As pointed out before, the financial plan will usefully be presented in a separate document. It should consist the following:

☐ Monthly financial plan
including monthly data for one historical year and at least two plan years.
- Summary of income statement and balance sheet, *Plansheets 1 and 2,* pages 108 and 109
- Income and expenditure, *Plansheets 3 to 10,* pages 111 to 123
- Investment and funding, *Plansheets 11 to 17,* pages 126 to 138
- Cash flow, *Plansheets 20 and 21,* pages 144 and 145

☐ Yearly financial plan
including yearly data for three historical years if available and five plan years. This should be the full-report version covering the information discussed in *Performing the projections,* page 106, as illustrated on *Plansheets 1 to 27,* specifically:
- Summary of income statement and balance sheet, *Plansheets 1 and 2,* pages 108 and 109
- Income and expenditure, *Plansheets 3 to 10,* pages 111 to 123
- Investment and funding, *Plansheets 11 to 17,* pages 126 to 138
- Financial structure, *Plansheets 18 and 19,* pages 140 and 141
- Cash flow and liquid reserves, *Plansheets 20 to 23,* pages 144 to 146
- Key financial indicators, *Plansheets 24 to 27,* pages 156 to 159

▌▌ *Brief, Precise, to the Point: The Exposé*

The exposé is a frequently used medium of preliminary communication. It does not pretend to convey sufficient information to support a decision or final judgement, but rather aims to create interest. In order to have that effect, your exposé needs to be short, ideally requiring no more than ten minutes for salient information to be absorbed. As a rule of thumb this means that it should not exceed a volume of ten pages, including attachments.

The following sample structure shows how the exposé is derived from the full-report version of your business plan.

Contents

Compare the corresponding sectors of the full-report version of the business plan outlined in Appendix I.

Corporate identity

☐ The firm
Legal entity: name, registered office, directors, chief executive officer, management, group affiliations, major shareholders, issued capital (as per the full-report version *1.1 The firm*, page 192), possibly expanded by extracts from *2.1 The firm and its shareholders*, page 193.

☐ History
Major developments and events that shaped the firm's present situation. (Extracts from *2.3 History of the firm and its business*, page 193 in the full-report version.)

Financial targets and requirements

☐ Major financial targets and return on capital
A small selection of plan statistics leading up to the projected returns on capital (as per the full-report version *1.3 Major financial targets and return on capital*, page 192), the table to include the last year of historical accounts and five plan years. The source of the data is the financial survey attached to the full-report version in a separate appendix (*Statistical appendix: Survey and analysis of financial data*, page 197) of which extracts are included in *Planned financial performance* on page 195. In the interest of readability, figure notation should be confined to significant digits.

> **Heads of tabulated financial targets**
> A sample selection
>
> > Equity
> > Debt
> > _____
> >
> > Total funds employed = total assets
> > *Equity ratio (%)*
> >
> > Sales revenue
> >
> > Number of employees
> >
> > Profit before interest and tax
> > *Return on sales (%)*
> >
> > **Return on assets *(%)***
> > (= Return on investment ROI)
> >
> > Profit before tax
> > ***Return on equity (%)***

☐ Requirement of resources and new finance sought
Concise listing of additional resources required for implementing the firm's strategy and the type and amount of the finance sought for the purpose (as per the full-report version *1.4 Requirement of resources and new finance sought*, page 192), possibly preceded by main conclusions of *3.3. Strategic targets*, page 194, *Strategic action plan*, page 195.

Operations

☐   The corporate mission
Summary of major statements, giving prominence to the items in bold type. (Compare the full-report version *3.3. Strategic targets*, page 194.)
  - General (long-term) policy goals
  - **Customer needs addressed**
  - **Product attributes**
  - **Target markets**
  - Essential operational technologies
  - Synergetic linkages
  - **Distinctive competences and resources**

☐   Product information
A very brief, preferably non-technical, product brochure might be attached to the exposé or, if not exceeding one or two pages, be inserted here.

☐   Management and organisation
Concise listings. (Compare the full-report version *2.2 Management and organisation*, page 193.)
  - **Management**
    The personalities of the executive team: name, qualifications, occupational career
  - **Operational organisation**
    Preferably summarised in an organisation chart identifying the areas of responsibility of the executives named in the preceding list

Success potential and strategy

Condensed, highlighting the items in bold type. (Compare the full-report version *3. Success potential and strategy*, page 193.)

☐   Market potential
  - Target markets and demand
  - Success conditions for suppliers
  - **Special competences of the firm**

☐   Competitive strength
  - Industry and supply conditions
  - Strengths and strategies of competitors
  - **Special competitive strengths of the firm**

☐   Strategic targets
  - The corporate mission
  - Main strategic thrusts
  - **Strategic action plan**

Planned financial performance

Source of the data is the comprehensive financial plan discussed in *Performing the projections*, page 106. For example, the plan data included could consist of the following three tables. If preferred, these might be condensed by aggregating sub-components. (Compare the full-report version *4.2 Planned financial performance*, page 195.)

☐ Financial plan summary
- Income statement, *Plansheet 1*, page 108
- Balance sheet, *Plansheet 2*, page 109
- Cash flow, *Plansheets 20 and 21*, pages 144 and 145, condensed into one page

☐ Key rating indicators
Optionally, a small selection of ratio indicators might be included, for example the four (or five) components of the Z-score formula together with the resulting score (see *Z-scoring your firm*, page 175).

III Your Calling Card: The Executive Overview

This is the shortest format into which your business plan might conceivably be compressed. It is the proverbial 'elevator pitch' made in writing, useful, in particular, in sounding out interest or preparing first contacts. Its format is very similar to the executive summary heading up the full-report version of the business plan. There is something to be said for preparing that summary such that it could be used, without change, for the purposes of a stand-alone overview. It is most effective if it is kept to one page and takes no more than two minutes to absorb.

Contents

Compare the corresponding sectors of the full-report version of the business plan outlined in Appendix I (page 189ff.).

The firm

As concise as possible: Name, registered office, directors, chief executive officer, management, group affiliations, major shareholders, issued capital (as per the full-report version *1.1 The firm*, page 192).

Major financial targets and return on capital

A small selection of plan statistics leading up to the projected returns on capital (as per the full-report version *1.3 Major financial targets and return on capital*, page 192), the table to include the last year of historical accounts and five plan years. In the interest of readability, figure notation should be confined to significant digits.

Heads of tabulated financial targets
A sample selection

> Equity
> Debt
>
> ———————————————
>
> Total funds employed = total assets
> *Equity ratio (%)*
>
> Sales revenue
>
> Number of employees
>
> Profit before interest and tax
> *Return on sales (%)*
>
> **Return on assets** *(%)*
> (= Return on investment ROI)
>
> Profit before tax
> **Return on equity** *(%)*

The corporate mission

Summary of major statements. (Compare the full-report version *3.3. Strategic targets*, page 194.) Focus on customer needs addressed, product attributes, target markets, distinctive competences and resources.

This the central item of the overview and should make full use of the remaining space.

Requirement of resources and new finance sought

Concise listing of additional resources required for implementing the firm's strategy and the type and amount of the finance sought for the purpose (as per the full-report version *1.4 Requirement of resources and new finance sought*, page 192).

Depending on the occasion for which the overview is intended, this item may be omitted to allocate more space to stating the firm's mission.

For Product Safety Concerns and Information please contact our EU
representative GPSR@taylorandfrancis.com Taylor & Francis Verlag GmbH,
Kaufingerstraße 24, 80331 München, Germany

Printed and bound by CPI Group (UK) Ltd, Croydon, CR0 4YY

01/05/2025

01858373-0001